The Roots
of Character

THE ROOTS *of* CHARACTER

Includes Character Development Exercises

ANTONIO L. MCDANIEL

AuthorHouse™
1663 Liberty Drive
Bloomington, IN 47403
www.authorhouse.com
Phone: 1-800-839-8640

© 2011 by Antonio L. McDaniel. All rights reserved.

No part of this book may be reproduced, stored in a retrieval system, or transmitted by any means without the written permission of the author.

First published by AuthorHouse   10/18/2011

ISBN: 978-1-4670-6183-4 (sc)
ISBN: 978-1-4670-6182-7 (hc)
ISBN: 978-1-4670-6181-0 (ebk)

Library of Congress Control Number: 2011918428

Printed in the United States of America

Any people depicted in stock imagery provided by Thinkstock are models, and such images are being used for illustrative purposes only.
Certain stock imagery © Thinkstock.

This book is printed on acid-free paper.

Because of the dynamic nature of the Internet, any web addresses or links contained in this book may have changed since publication and may no longer be valid. The views expressed in this work are solely those of the author and do not necessarily reflect the views of the publisher, and the publisher hereby disclaims any responsibility for them.

Dedication

To my Heavenly Father, who sent His Son Jesus just for me.

To my darling wife, Phyllis, who taught me that by making yourself vulnerable, you actually become strong.

To my sons, Ryan and Corban, who remind me, through imitating my actions that I must continue to develop and gravitate toward God.

To my parents, Harry and Annette McDaniel, who were responsible for introducing me to God and encouraging my commitment to the Lord.

To one of God's great, HRM Kingsley Fletcher, who is responsible for causing me not to become comfortable with salvation, but rather to seek intimacy with God for the sake of His people.

Finally, to all those who need to be reminded that substance is greater than form and that God chooses those with developing roots.

Contents

Dedication v
Acknowledgments ix
Foreword xi

Chapters

1. Building for Character 1
2. The Roots of Love 12
3. The Roots of Vision 26
4. The Roots of a Renewed Mind 33
5. The Roots of Giving 41
6. The Roots of Faith and Wisdom 49
7. The Roots of Discipline 68
8. The Roots of Impartation 84
9. The Roots of Leadership 95
10. The Roots of Development 105
11. Remembering your Roots 112
12. The Beginning 122
13. Character Development Exercises 129

Acknowledgments

The Roots of Character is written as a testimony to God; though there are still areas that need polishing, my life is indicative of what God can do in anyone who desires Him. It is written to say thanks to Jesus Christ, who makes it all possible. His intercession allows me to express to God the compassion of my heart, even though I can do nothing to earn this right. It is written to my Counselor, the Holy Spirit, who was leading and guiding me, even when I did not know Him.

Also, *The Roots of Character* is written to express gratitude to God's number one agent of change and development in my life, my wife, Phyllis. Often, it amazed me how she always seemed to know what God was saying or wanted to say. Her connection with God was so profound, at times she did not have to speak or say anything and the expressions on her face were as is if God was physically before me. Please, do not let my satire interfere with the appreciation of my wife's unyielding commitment and support. I am constantly reassured that she was taken from my ribs as I breathe a little easier every day just knowing that she is beside me. I thank God for this gift He has given me. My hope is that I live my life being full of the character of God to express the appreciation I have for her.

Finally, *The Roots of Character* is written to as an inheritance to my sons, Ryan and Corban. As I am discovering more about God, I am reminded that love has no boundaries as I interact with my sons. My hope for them is that I will be an example of godliness and that my character will encourage them to pursue a personal relationship and intimacy with God.

Foreword

A fingerprint, a smile and even tastes in music are trademarks that distinguish individuals from one another, giving us identity. Such is the case with character building. Each of us has faced unique or "trademark" experiences that have attributed to our moral fiber or who we really are. In his book, The Roots of Character, Antonio McDaniel takes us on a journey of how character is formulated. This writing is a line upon line, precept upon precept teaching that provokes us to take a closer look at ourselves and the temperament we display. The Body of Christ will benefit from the wealth of knowledge shared in this book. I highly recommend it.

HRM Kingsley A. Fletcher
Pastor, Life Community Church
Research Triangle Park, North Carolina

Introduction

A beautiful plant blossoms and brings pleasure to all who see it. Whether friend or foe to the planter, it would not matter to the plant as it gives off the breath of life to those who cross its paths. This breath of life or scientifically, photosynthesis, is the process by which green plants and certain other organisms use the energy of light to convert carbon dioxide and water into the simple sugar glucose; the resulting byproduct of photosynthesis is oxygen, on which most organisms depend. This glucose is produced in overabundance and is then stored in the roots, stems and leaves for later use. Like people, plants do not discriminate as to who can benefit from its natural growth and development, but humbly fulfills its purpose and helps make life a little easier for everyone. As you observe and appreciate the plant for its generosity, you may want to share the blessings of this plant. Therefore, with a skillful hand a piece of the plant is removed for the purpose of reproducing after its own kind. However, the offspring of the plant is not placed in dirt and expected to immediately produce the breath of life; there is a process, a natural order that must be followed.

  Before the plant can produce life, its foundation must be solidified; its life line must be established. Often the plant would be set in water such that the plant's desire to produce life would manifest itself. Out of the stem of the plant that was cut, its roots would come forth. These roots would function as organs of absorption, not only to keep the plant alive while in water, but also as its anchor of support when placed in dirt. Although the roots are being formed and have the ability to sustain life, until the stem and roots are placed in the dirt, it can not produce life.

Introduction

For example, an African violet, a smooth and adoring plant with deep green petals and majestic like flowers, easily produces roots, but unless it is put in dirt no lasting result will come forth; the stem or leaf of the African violet that is used to reproduce life will actually lose its life. In reality, I should say *give* its life, so that others may live. This is what Jesus meant in John 12:24-25 (NIV), when He said that "The seed that falls to the ground must die in order to produce life; the man who loves his life will lose it, while the man who hates his life in this world will keep it for eternal life."

    A plant's source of strength is its roots; no roots, no tree; no tree, no fruit; no fruit, leads to false expectations and may result in being cursed; remember in Matthew 11:12-14 when Jesus cursed the fig tree. The bible says that Jesus was hungry and saw the fig tree in leaf—in leaf means that it had the appearance of fruit; at a minimum it should have had buds or baby fruit; He checked it out and found nothing but leaves and cursed it. This curse was not because Jesus was hungry and could not eat, but due to the fig tree's *deception*. It would have been better if the tree had no leaves on it at all. The fig tree is a metaphor for our attitude and character; one should not merely have the appearance of commitment and dedication, i.e., fruit bearing, but rather demonstrate through discipline the necessary commitment to be successful in the Kingdom of God. Nonetheless, at the core of the fig tree's non productivity, is an undeveloped root system that was not capable of fulfilling its purpose. The fig tree's roots were only deep enough to energize it, but were not deep enough to produce in substance. In other words, the fig tree appeared as it had fruit and was able to provide nourishment to sustain life in actuality it did not. For emphasis, again I say, the curse of the fig tree was not about the fruit; the curse came because it deceptively looked as if it had fruit. Since the fig tree misrepresented itself, it was considered to be undependable and therefore received its just reward. Likewise, there are many who have the energy to volunteer

The Roots of Character

and shout "Here I am Lord, send me," but where is the fruit? Where is the needed discipline to accomplish the task? What is at the core of this inconsistency? What is the prohibitive factor? Why has stagnation become a motto? What preempts a vision and cements lack? Keep these questions in mind as the discussion progresses from roots to trees.

A tree is a woody perennial plant having a single usually elongated main stem generally with few or no branches on its lower part. Without regard to your literal location or physical address, you need trees. Simply, trees are big plants that produce or give off oxygen. Trees take in carbon dioxide and release oxygen; people take in oxygen and give off carbon dioxide. Humans are partners with trees. Trees, through its roots, absorb water from the earth and release it back into the air and therefore help to cool the earth. This moisture leads to more rain and the rain provides the water all living things need. See, everything supports and feeds off of each other; to borrow a line from one of my son's animated movies, "This is the cycle of life." Notwithstanding, in addition to being a valuable asset in its natural state, trees are also valuable in producing many of our daily resources. The words in this book are printed on materials that came from trees; trees allow us to play with baseball bats, to stay warm when burned for heat and even to rest as it is used in furniture. There are thousands of things made from trees. However, the greatest thing this valuable and renewable resource is used for is building. Most notably, King Solomon, son of David, used the cypress and pine trees to build the temple of the Lord and Noah used cypress wood to build the ark that was to preserve life on earth. In addition to being used to build, trees carried with them a sign that God was indeed with His people.

In Isaiah 41:19, the prophet Isaiah, gives this word, "I will put in the desert the cedar and the acacia, the myrtle and the olive. I will set pines in the wasteland, the fir and the cypress together, so that people may see and know,

Introduction

may consider and understand, that the hand of the Lord has done this, that the Holy One of Israel has created it." More specifically, in this same Isaiah, beginning around the fortieth chapter and continuing through midway of chapter 56, Isaiah is prophesying about God's divine deliverance being assured for His people; the prophesy reaches its climax in Isaiah 55:13, "Instead of the thorn bush will grow the pine tree, and instead of briers the myrtle will grow." Now, Isaiah had just spoken the word that God's word will not return to Him void. So, since God said it, it will be; correction, if God said it, then it is! From the middle of chapter 56 through the end of the Book of Isaiah, the prophecies that come forth relate to the final establishment of God's kingdom. These words are recorded in Isaiah 60:13, "The glory of Lebanon will come to you, the pine, the fir and the cypress together, to adorn the place of my sanctuary; and I will glorify the place of my feet." In order to understand what God is truly saying, you have to look at the trees, specifically, those that are repeatedly mentioned, the myrtle, the pine, and the cypress trees; for emphasis the cedar and fir tress are included.

The pine, cypress, fir and cedar are all evergreen trees; each one has different shaped leaves and may or may not have cones. These trees are valued for their shade, ornament and wood. Unique to the pine tree, is that it yields a resinous sap that is used to produce turpentine and pine tar. Pine tar is used to make pitch; pitch is used to water proof wood (remember Noah's ark). Specific to the Cedar is that it has more durable, aromatic and often reddish woods of Cedar. Cedar trees are native to the Old World, such as the Cedar of Lebanon. In Isaiah 60:13, *the glory of Lebanon* is a direct reference to the Cedar of Lebanon. The glory of Lebanon is its trees! The myrtle is one of several evergreen shrubs or trees; it is an aromatic shrub native to the Mediterranean, having pink or white flowers. In Leviticus 23:37-43, the Word is describing what is to happen concerning the Feast of Tabernacles. "These are the Lord's appointed feasts, which you are to proclaim

The Roots of Character

as sacred assemblies for bringing offerings and grain offerings, sacrifices and drink offerings required for each day. These offerings are in addition to those for the Lord's Sabbaths and in addition to your gifts and whatever you have vowed and all freewill offerings you give to the Lord. So beginning with the fifteenth day of the seventh month, after you have gathered the crops of the land, celebrate the festival of the Lord for seven days; the first day is a day of rest, and the eighth day also is a day of rest. On the first day you are to take choice fruits from the trees, and palm fronds, leafy branches and poplars, and rejoice before the Lord your God for seven days. Celebrate this as a festival to the Lord for seven days each year. This is to be lasting ordinance for the generations to come; celebrate it in the seventh month. Live in booths for seven days: All native born Israelites are to live in booths so that your descendants will know that I had the Israelites live booths when I brought them out of Egypt. I am the Lord your God." These booths that the Israelites were to live in to celebrate the goodness of God were made from the myrtle and were designed to be a place of rest. In Genesis 33:17, we find Jacob, after journeying to Succoth, built himself a house and made booths or places of shelter for his livestock.

In connecting the prophecies using the trees with the definition and purpose of those trees, then I am forced to conclude that in the driest of all deserts, when there appears to be no more life, God will set pines before you so that you may build; when it seems impossible for anything but disaster to manifest, God will show his glory and everyone will know that He's God! Also, instead of briers and the thorn bush that tear down or cause discomfort, the Lord will give you the pine tree and myrtle; He will cause you to build and give you rest. Additionally, for any condition that has plagued you or an aroma that has caused a stench, it will be replaced by the fragrance of the cedar, your life shall be reestablished by His strength and you shall glorify Him in His sanctuary! Praise the Lord!

Introduction

Despite His wonder, God respects the laws of nature and therefore in order for all these great and wonderful trees to manifest, the roots have to be in place. Yet again, nothing can grow and produce without established roots. Without roots there is no glory; without roots the pine and myrtle trees can only dream of building a house or allowing rest; without roots all hope to weather storms is lost. A heavy downpour that would have fed and strengthened, now only washes away. Unless the foundation is established or the support is cemented or the roots are deep, any measure of greatness is reduced to ashes in a fire. At the core of this greatness is character.

As such, if you were a tree and your life is the fruit, could you be used to build God's house? Do the roots of your character provide support? Are you able to maintain your footing when blind sided? Can God depend on you to service His kingdom? He can and apparently you have a strong desire to be dependable to Him; this is why God caused you and the principles in this book to cross paths. As you read and study this book, you may start to feel a little uncomfortable and agitated; you may shift frequently in your chair; or you may even be tempted to toss it aside (hopefully, you will resist). As you have these growth experiences, my prayer is that you will realize that your roots are growing and allow the Holy Spirit to minister to your heart as He prepares you for greatness.

Greatness is typified by your service to God and His people. Jesus said, "I did not come to be served, but to serve." There is no question as to His greatness. I remember, as I was graduating from school, that one of my instructors wrote in my yearbook, "I dare you to be great!" Initially, I thought that this was a cute expression to write in a yearbook; I did not realize nor embrace the full impact of those words until years later. The book was destroyed in a flood, but those words were written on my heart as much as they written on the inside cover of my yearbook. Those words had and continue to have a profound impact on my life. Today, I can profess greatness, not because I have or have done anything, but because I understand and apply the principle that to be great one must serve. This writing is a testimony of greatness, in that I am serving you with what God has given me. My hope is that you too will become great!

Building for Character

It has more value than the anointing and the anointing breaks yokes; it has more depth than love and love covers a multitude of sin; it has more substance than faith and without faith it is impossible to please Him; embracing or imitating the character of Christ is the focal point for breaking yokes, covering sin and pleasing God. I hope that at the core of every Christian's faith would be the personal desire to become like Christ. Jesus should be at the center of our being and the inspiration to our every act; without Christ there is nothing and without Him, we are nothing. My desire is to provoke and encourage you join me in the pursuit of the character of Christ. This notion is way beyond a slogan on a wrist band or t-shirt; beyond the pop culture phenomenon of *WWJD* or *What would Jesus do?* How would one know what Jesus would do, if they do not know Jesus? Understand this, Jesus did not consider equality with God as something to hold, but made Himself nothing for us. He humbled Himself and became obedient, even to the point of death.

Jesus' ministry reflected and showed mankind who we can become by abiding totally in Him; this includes the ability to be completely selfless. His attitude was full of love and compassion; everything He did, He did for someone else. This embodies the essence of the Son of God; it reflects the true character of who man is to become. We are to be Christ's ambassadors; His representatives of the Kingdom of God in the earth. The ability to effectively walk in an ambassadorship rests with having a working knowledge and firm understanding of the kingdom or country you represent. For example, the ambassador of the United States is able to walk on foreign

Building for Character

soil as if he or she is still walking in the U.S. If someone were to touch this ambassador, whoever would be touching the United States and thereby creating an international incident. See, an ambassador walks with the full weight of the country or government behind him (or her). Every step taken and every word spoken by the ambassador is a direct reflection of the country represented. Now consider that the bible records in 1 Corinthians 5:20a, "We are therefore ambassadors of Christ . . ." So our words and actions should reflect Christ as we represent Him on earth to His people. For emphasis, an ambassador of Christ must think, speak, and act in a manner that is consistent with and reflective of the values of the Kingdom of God; at the root of this is the absorption of the character of the Kingdom into the mindset of the representative. Simply stated, to be like Jesus, you have to know Jesus; you have to know His character in order to mirror His character.

The development of your character requires time alone with God. Psalms 91:1-3 reads, "He who dwells in the secret place of the Most High will rest in the shadow of the Almighty. I will say of the Lord, 'He is my refuge and my fortress, my God in whom I trust'" and in Isaiah 48:17a "This is what the Lord says—your Redeemer, the Holy One of Israel: 'I am the Lord your God, who teaches you what is best for you, who directs you in the way you should go." These scripture references are key components to the foundation of character. It is obvious that the more you want from God, the more time you have to spend with Him. No matter how good a teacher is, it is impossible to be taught unless you go and be attentive in class. *Class* is defined as the opening of your mind to new opportunities or possibilities in realizing the magnitude of God.

Your mind is the classroom and there is always a lesson to be learned and applied. Psalms 27:11-14 reads, "Teach me your way, O Lord; lead me in a straight path because of my oppressors. Do not turn me over to the desire of my foes, for false witnesses rise up against me, breathing out violence. I am still confident of this: I will see the goodness of the Lord in the land of the living. Wait for the Lord; be strong and take heart and wait for the Lord." This notion is not as complex or as demanding as it appears; the bible already tells us to study to show yourself approved. Paraphrased, the bible states that you are to die daily to self and to beat your body daily and gain control of yourself so that you will not be disqualified for the prize after you have preached to others. In other words, practice what you preach. This concept alludes to the development of both the spiritual and natural man.

There should be a balance between the spiritual and natural. It is true that a man who gains the world and loses his soul has not succeeded and has not done himself any good. The paradox is that the opposite is also true. The man, who gains all spiritual things and has no earthly basis, is no earthly good. It is absolutely irritating to talk to someone who can not relate to you on a personal level. Everything out of their mouth is Amen, Praise the Lord; frequently, they change up, then it is Praise the Lord, Amen. It is reasonable and expected that one develops in their relationship and knowledge of God for the purpose of capitalizing on this relation to win souls to Christ; remember, as an ambassador, we are required and should see God and spirituality in everything; whether or not we talk about it or inject this revelation in an ongoing conversation could be the difference between successfully getting a soul saved and looking like a religious fanatic. God is in everything and there is a lesson to be learned in all things, however, people become so wrapped up in having the appearance of spirituality that they can not do God any good. If you lose or do not have the ability to connect with someone, to walk them through their difficult times, then they may not get to God because they are trying to get away from you. In this regard, there is no balance.

On the subject of balance, Moses would enter the presence of God as he went inside the tent of meeting. However, he did not remain inside the tent. Moses had to come out of His tangible presence and walk in the assurances

Building for Character

associated with carrying out God's plan. Likewise, you should be able to enter into the presence of God, but realize you are not going to stay there; you should be able to lead your family in spiritual things, but not every single moment of the day. You do not need the power and anointing of the Holy Spirit to enjoy putt putt golf or a scoop of ice cream. For anyone who may be reading this and thinking that the bible says to *pray without ceasing,* allow me to put this in context. To pray without ceasing does not mean to pray twenty four hours a day, seven days a week; it means that when the Lord lays a burden on your heart and is prompting you to pray (maybe even waking you in the middle of the night), you should not tell the Lord how tired you are. At these times, you pray without ceasing until you sense a legitimate release in the spirit concerning the prayer.

Nonetheless, balance is relatively difficult to obtain and even more difficult to maintain. You can not truly lead in spiritual things and your natural life falters; this is like telling your creditor, of whom you consistently pay late (if at all), that God is your provider. Imagine your Pastor, leading prayer, preaching the Word of God, praying for the sick, but then neglecting his family as it relates to spousal or parental responsibilities. This Pastor would be run out of town in the name of hypocrisy. There has to be balance; remember, before Jesus died on the cross, He gave His mother to John's care. I do not know where Joseph was (most likely he had died), but Jesus made natural provisions for His mother before completing His spiritual work.

Conceptually, balance does not mean equality; this is not about fifty-fifty or ten things getting 10% of your time. Balance means to establish a priority over your life and with those priorities create a measure or basis for fulfillment. For example, I was helping to clean up a building that would eventually become our church facility. The building was a mess and needed to be prepared for church service the next day. Around 6:30 p.m. on Saturday evening I would engage in a simple, but profound conversation that would impact the rest of my life. I was telling a brother in Lord that I had been at the church from around 9:00 a.m. He briefly shared his testimony and then said, "It is not your responsibility to clean this whole church." It was then that I realized that no matter how much I personally did, there was always going to be more given the size of the project. I concluded that nine and one half hours on a Saturday was enough of a reasonable service and left to go spend time with my wife. To simplify this further, balance is recognizing that more than one thing is important and whereas, we are encouraged to be all things to all people, we can not do everything for everybody. Plainly, there are some Saturdays when only one hour is a reasonable service; even more, there are times when it is more expedient to stay home; as long as your heart is right and you are not contrary to God's will, your greatest service really could be at your home. I learned this lesson that day and it has been a part of me ever sense.

See, I am and will always be a student. My thirst for knowledge is not just for me, but for those to whom I come in contact. Due to a desire to share that which I come to understand, the knowledge obtained must be proven, especially as it relates to God. Loud authoritative statements, no matter how reasonable or sound, are not and do not become the gospel; actually, if it is not written in the bible, then it may be not the gospel. Acts 17:11 reads, "Now the Bereans were of more noble character than the Thessalonians, for they received the message with great eagerness and examined the Scriptures every day to see if what Paul said was true." Relying solely on what someone says concerning biblical principles, without proving them as a person of integrity in God, is unwise and dangerous to the spiritual and natural man. Since Jesus is the final authority, whether there is confidence or a lack of confidence or comfort in whoever is sharing information, you should exercise your personal responsibility to search the scriptures to validate the word for yourself. By obtaining this assurance, even if it turns out that the uneasy feeling is conviction by the Holy Spirit, or

Building for Character

soundly rejecting a teaching that proves to be false, you are deepening your relationship with God and therefore will expedite your growth in Him. I do caution you, do not immediately conclude that a hard teaching is wrong or antichrist and automatically reject it. Take the time to study and find out for yourself; allow the Holy Spirit to minister to you; to comfort you (if needed) or provide the needed assurances concerning your position as required.

It is also necessary to be proactive in reading and studying the Word or any other material that stimulates the spirit man and promotes growth. 2 Timothy 2:15 says, "Do your best to present yourself to God as one approved, a workman who does not need to be ashamed and who correctly handles the Word of truth." However, you should not just read to prove or disprove the accuracy of statements; instead, read and study to show yourself approved by God for the building of your relationship with him. Let your search for knowledge be part of your reasonable service. As you move forward in development, the day will come when you will have to stand alone. This day of reckoning, as I call it, is the day when you are a majority of one. This is the day when all you have learned, understand and apply to your life is challenged in ways that you could not even imagine. This is the day that the principles on which you stand, cause you to stand by yourself. The depth of your conviction and righteous will be revealed; this is the time when all your experience and courage will be tried and tested. This period will not be about those with whom you contend, but about what you believe. As recorded in 2 Timothy 3:16, "At my first defense, no one came to my support, but everyone deserted me. May it not be held against them." You will be tested not only on your belief in God, but also on what you have learned about yourself. This is where true balance is measured. This is not the point of no return, but more so this could be a point of spiraling confusion or limited progress. Keep in mind, the test you have not passed is the one you keep taking.

The Roots of Character

Psalms 34:19-20 reads, "A righteous man may have many troubles, but the Lord delivers him from them all; He protects all his bones, not one of them will be broken." Into each life a little rain must fall; at times, it seems like it rains only when you want to have a picnic. Without question the storms of life are coming; the only thing in question is whether you will be ready for them. When you know a specific storm is coming, it is wonderful to prepare for it and successfully mitigate the difficulties of these trials. Overcoming great tests would be an accomplishment and should be commended. However, the greater test or trial and tribulation period comes when you do not have advanced warning or the chance to prepare. I Peter 2:19 reads, "For it is commendable if a man bears up under the pain of unjust suffering because he is conscious of God." This is why God says to meditate on His word day and night and to be ready in season and out of season.

In 1999, a hurricane approached the Carolinas from the Atlantic and every news program was reporting that this storm was going to be the strongest, most damaging hurricane to hit the Carolina region. On this basis, everyone was prepared for it; all the milk and eggs had sold out, businesses closed down and boarded up, all lose items where either tied down or taken inside; we were ready! I imagine that everyone who knew how to pray and even those who did not were talking to God about this storm with the hopes that its path would be diverted or for it to subside. Suffice it to say the storm turned away from the Carolinas and skirted up the east coast. Seemingly, all the preparation was for naught as prayers were answered, but then the storm did an interesting thing. Instead of continuing up the coast, it turned and made it way back to North Carolina. The winds had died down, but that was no longer the problem. This storm seemed to have a mind of its own and was bent on destruction; there was so much rain from this degraded hurricane that cities were literally flooded out. The new reports showed people on top of their homes trying to avoid the rising water. This

Building for Character

flood was reminiscent of the flood in Noah's day; thank God for the rainbow. I am not sure how any one could prepare for a resurgent storm like this; the losses included homes, cars and other property; those who had understanding, thanked God for their life but still may have wept bitterly and became angry over their misfortune. It truly was a difficult time and expected events since the storm has seemingly passed by.

Floods, accidents, deaths, or any other event that could prove to be greatly destructive or tragic, happen suddenly. If you know someone is terminally ill and about to die you can prepare for it and will most likely accept and deal with the loss a whole lot better than if someone dies unexpectedly. Nonetheless, it is within these sudden experiences that it is necessary to remember that the Lord will deliver you from all troubles. When you are ready to give up and your voice can no longer cry out. You may ask, "What did I do to deserve this?" or "Why is this happening?" God will remind you that this present suffering is nothing compared to the glory to be revealed. Your conversation with the Lord may become a little jaded; as in Lord when I think I am moving along and progressing toward happiness, I get hit again. Why? God reminds you that to suffer unjustly is to suffer as Christ and that as you suffer with Him you shall reign with Him. This is the point where you have to determine what is *unjust* and what is foolishness brought on by human error.

To have severe pains and trials, because of bad decision making is not suffering as Christ suffered; to continue to live and exist in a depraved state because of a refusal to grow and change, leads to a suffering that is not based on Christ, but instead is a result of poor judgment. It is not wise to continue to put God in the position of deliverer when He has already made every provision for you. God says to call upon Him in the day of trouble and He will answer you. God does not want you to continue to call upon Him for the same trouble over and over again. In the Book of Judges the Israelites, in the absence of strong leadership, would revert to detestable and corruptible practices; these acts resulted in God's judgment and the enslavement of the Israelites. This pattern of sin, slavery, prayer, deliverance, sin, slavery, prayer, deliverance repeated itself for generations. They did not learn the lessons from their forefathers and therefore did not stay the course and needed to be repeatedly delivered. This was not pleasing to God. Likewise, if you were in, say, financial bondage and God allowed you to get free only to have you end up in financial bondage again, the question is not whether God will free you, but rather the question to ask yourself is "Am I pleasing Him?" God would free you because He is a faithful God who will not deny Himself as such, just like he continued to deliver the Israelites from themselves, he will deliver you as well. God's intent for you is to learn from your mistakes and more importantly, to not repeat them. Keep in mind, you will have enough trials, without creating any for yourself.

Notwithstanding, there is a notion of development that happens even when the storm is selfgenerated. Perhaps to some degree a greater development happens with selfgenerated storms because at some point you realize that you caused it. Therefore, the consequences are a result of your decision making or actions and you are completely responsible without an outlet for blame. Always remember that some of the most insightful lessons learned usually result from an error in judgment. God says that "blessed is he who perseveres under trial . . ." Be mindful, this is not a license to be ignorant; you are accountable for your actions. It is to say that you are human and will make mistakes; just be prepared for the consequences. One of the most peculiar things about life is that it actually waits until we flunk the course and then teaches us the lesson.

I use to teach at a bible college in North Carolina; one day I was conversing with a potential student who had expressed a strong interest in taking the course on leadership that I was teaching, but emphatically stated that she would not be taking it. I did ask the obvious

Building for Character

question of "why?" She proceeded to explain what happens to her physical body at the notion of taking tests. For the record and what will be apparent when I tell you what she told me, we do have a relationship beyond teacher and student. As described, this condition has been with her throughout her schooling and for her, had become a good excuse not to continue in academics or any other form of development that requires testing. At the thought of having to take a test, she not only begins to perspire like an athlete in training but will also develop diarrhea. Obviously, this affects her ability to concentrate (on the tests); her ability to do well is compromised because she has to spend more time in the *rest*room as opposed to studying. I use to occasionally wonder, since life is a test, does she have permanent diarrhea? It is an unfortunate situation that she is in as a result of this mental bondage. I am not a psychiatrist, but this one is easy. I hope she reads this book and realizes that by limiting her development to avoid diarrhea (or any discomfort), she is also restricting her growth. When something is suppose to grow and does not, then it gets cursed; remember the fig tree? If only she would realize that there is nothing strange or uncommon about tests; that tests do not have power but merely reflect the discipline someone has put forth.

Additionally, tests are merely feats to prove understanding or completion of certain aspects of your development. God says to prove Him, just so He can demonstrate that He is who He says He is. Malachi 3:10 reads, "Bring the whole tithe into the storehouse, that there may be food in my house. 'Test me in this', says the Lord Almighty, 'and see if I will not throw open the floodgates of heaven and pour out so much blessing that you will not have room enough for it.'" Since the Creator of the world, says to test him to prove Himself and since Job who had become full of the righteousness of God was abundantly tested, how common is it to man to experience such things? The bible records these words in James 1:2-3, "consider it pure joy, my brothers, whenever you face trials of many kinds, because you know that the testing of your faith develops perseverance" and then in verse 12, "blessed is the man who perseveres under trial. Because when he has stood the test, he will receive the crown of life." To say that tests are normal is a gross understatement. Tests are necessary for growth and development; without tests, there is no evidence of understanding; without tests, there is no demonstration that you are ready for more and without tests, there is no testimony.

The elements required for building your character, fellowship with God, reading His Word, enduring crisis and tests, all have a primary component. This component is time. It takes time to development character, especially character that is to be Christ like. By definition a Christian is one who *manifests the qualities or spirit of Christ*. Implicit to this definition is the notion of consistency. Hence, a Christian would have to consistently manifest the qualities or Spirit of Christ. Personally, I am not 100% consistent and thus will more commonly refer to myself as a disciple. My goal is to be a Christian by the implicit definition, but I am not there yet; as a disciple, I am learning how to obtain Christianity. Christians are affirmed after their character in Christ is established and again, character building is a process of time. For many this book will cement you in your Christ likeness but for others it will become the foundation. The following chapters denote the roots to which your foundation should be built; for with this foundation, there is nothing that you can not overcome.

The Roots of Love

As recorded in 1 John 1:1-2, "In the beginning was the Word, and the Word was with God, and the Word was God. He was with God in the beginning." Then in verse 14, "The Word became flesh and made his dwelling among us." To put this in context, when Jesus was in heaven with God, He was the Word; hence, in Genesis 1:26, when God says "Let us make man in our image" He was talking to Word and the Spirit of the Word, the Holy Spirit. The bible also states in 1 John 4:16, that God is Love. Since God is Love and the Word was God, it is easy to conclude that the Word is Love. Likewise, as the bible encourages the reading, studying, understanding and application of the Word, it is not a great leap to say that you should read, study, understand and apply love.

Jesus' decision to redeem mankind was a great sacrifice. Relatively speaking, it would have been easier for Jesus to go to the cross as the Lamb of God, if He did not have to separate from God to do so. In order for man to be redeemed the sins or darkness of the world had to come upon Him. Since dark and light can not simultaneously occupy the same place, Jesus had to separate Himself from God. This is what Jesus was referring to when He asked God "Why have you forsaken me?" Through it all, we are here today and able to praise God for what He has done. "For God so loved the world, He gave His only begotten Son . . ." as recorded in John 3:16. Love was epitomized through Jesus on the cross.

As it relates to our walk with God, the manifestation of love occurs in many ways. I vividly recall the day when the overzealousness of a five or six year, caused me to mistakenly put spicy barbecue sauce on my French fries;

The Roots of Character

without any hesitation, my mother had taken my fries and had given me hers. This example shows the simple nature to which love is uncovered. A greater example of this demonstration by my mother occurs as I was still in her womb. The pregnancy with me was a difficult one; there were several complications, including high blood pressure and kidney problems. If that were the end of it, maybe things would not have been so bad. However, in the sixth month of an already complicated and trying pregnancy, a tumor was discovered on my forehead; to put this in perspective, if my head was the size of a softball, then the tumor had grown to the size of a tennis ball. The doctors told my mother that based on the size of the tumor and other issues that "It would be best if the pregnancy was terminated." Not only was there high blood pressure, kidney failure, and the growing tumor, but also the position of the tumor was equally as detrimental. It was growing over my forehead and would possibly grow over my nose and eventually suffocate me (if I made it through the pregnancy); furthermore, if she were to lay on her back or if I shifted the wrong way, I could press against her heart and stop it from beating. To the doctors and nurses, it appeared as if this were a no win situation. My mother did not have the relationship with God then that she has now, but she did have a gift from God by way of her stubbornness; it was a gift to me anyway!) My mother at this point decided that the doctors no longer had her best interest in mind and stopped going; actually, she did not trust them and felt as though they were going to force or deceive her into aborting. Again, this was the sixth month; for the next three months my mother had to sleep upright, as if she were in a chair. Every attempt to get her to go to the doctor or to sway her failed; praise and thank God for the gift of stubbornness! The following months were increasingly difficult, but she stayed the course; then one day, as she walked through the house she collapsed into my father's arms. My mother can not recall any of the specifics from the time she collapsed and four

The Roots of Love

days later when she held her son in her arms. I was named Antonio; the literal meaning of that name is "priceless" for after all she had gone through that is what I was to her. However, I was not out of the woods yet; the doctor's said that I would not live my past two years due to the kidney failure. My mother's failed kidneys caused excess waste to remain in her body, and this resulted in my blood being poisoned. Again my mother came through for me; once a week for the three months, my mother's blood (she had recovered) was taken from her and used to give me blood transfusions. As her renewed blood was given to me, it pushed out the poisonous blood that was inside of me. This is what my mother did for me and why in my heart, every day is Mother's Day. I had heard my mother called stubborn and had actually begun to accept the description of her until I was told this story; I concluded that she was not really stubborn, but determined to show God's love. We have always had a unique and special bond and now it is cemented even more because like my mother I want to be stubborn for Jesus!

Love, for the purpose of this writing, is defined as the *denial of self* and in its purest form demands selfless acts; however, with poetic license, I dare to say that the true essence of love is rooted in selfish behavior. I know it sounds crazy but keep reading and it will begin to make sense. The following is an excerpt of a poem I wrote:

> I give you my life because it makes me happy
> > And I want to be full of joy
> It is your laughter that makes my heartbeat
> > And I want my blood to flow
> Assurance comes when you call my name
> > And I want you to depend on me
> When I see you hurting, I feel the pain
> > And I do not like to ache
> I feed you because you nourish me
> > And I want to continue to grow

> I get your blanket because you keep me warm
> > And I don't like to be cold
> Holding your hand makes me feel safe
> > And I want security
>
> Because I want for me, I love you!

Selfishly, I do for you because it makes me feel good. I am sure you have had the occasion to show great kindness and love to someone who did not show any appreciation; you were not discouraged because you did it out of love. The energy released in kindness becomes its own reward because in your heart you know you did the right thing and that God would be pleased with your actions. As stated in scripture, whatever you do, do it with all your heart, for this is a reasonable service unto the Lord. The lack of appreciation shown has nothing to do with what God requires of you; when God impresses acts of love on your heart, it is your obedience that matters not whether someone acknowledges your kindness.

1 Corinthians 13:4-8 reads "Love is patient, love is kind. It does not envy, it does not boast, it is not proud. It is not rude, it is not selfseeking, it is not easily angered, and it keeps no record of wrongs. Love does not delight in evil, but rejoices with the truth. It always trusts, always hopes, and always perseveres. Love never fails." This means that love causes you to humbly and gently take time to stay calm and minister the same grace and mercy ministered to you by God; also, just as God does not hold our sins against Him against us, neither should we keep a diary, literally or figuratively, of how people have wrong us. Love covers a multitude of sin, including the sin against you. Simply put, love is also forgiveness.

One of the most difficult acts of love to show is forgiveness; this situation is unfortunate because it leads to such personal despair and hardening of the heart. Unforgivingness envelops your heart like a blanket; effectively restricting your blood flow and ultimately

The Roots of Love

cutting short your life. For a moment, imagine the worst thing that someone could do to you or your loved one. Like most I am sure things like murder, rape, adultery, molestation, abuse, etc. would come to mind. Now compare those things to the things that you have done against God. In case you are thinking that this is not the same, consider this, God says that anger in the heart is like murder; also, if you lust after someone, it is as if you have already committed adultery. The worst things that could happen to us, we do to God every day and yet, God forgives us. His mercy is renewed every morning. Despite every act of disobedience, sins known and unknown (or yet to be revealed), we awake the next day with a new basket of mercy, that is woven by grace. I am not inferring that forgiveness is always easy but am saying that forgiveness is required of us. Jesus references this as He was teaching His disciples how to pray; he said, "If you forgive those who trespass against you, your Heavenly Father will also forgive you. But if you do not forgive their sins, your Father will not forgive your sins."

Forgiveness is not about the other person but is about you and the attitude of your heart. Holding on to grudges not only leads to bitterness but also preempts the blessings of God from freely flowing in your life. Love through forgiveness is a powerful weapon against the enemy. One of the things the devil uses against children of God is their past. Often all the wrong, the sin, the lies will come to your mind at seemingly the strangest times; actually it is a well-timed attack. At a time to what the devil would call opportune, the devil will also bring to your mind all the hurt, the pain, the frustration, the loneliness, the anger, the bitterness, the despair, the bullies; anything that will cause you to take your eyes off God is fair game to the devil. It would be great if God would save our minds when we ask Him to enter our hearts. Unfortunately, He does not, however He has given us the weapon of forgiveness to destroy the devil's ability to use our past against us. Since

The Roots of Character

your memory will remain, even though your mind is renewed, you must use this weapon to keep focused on God.

This is not to say that you have to relive and confess sin by sin, but if the devil is using those things against you, then it is an area where you need to confess and repent in order to take back that area of your mind. For example, an area where this notion hits home for me is with the neighborhood bully; actually, he was not the neighborhood's bully, this was my own personal bully. To my knowledge, I was the only one he picked on. I tried my best never to be around him unless there were other people around, specifically my brothers or his sisters. Since that was not always the case I often became the target of his hatred toward me. I remember the helplessness that I felt but more so I remember the anger. Every time this came to my mind I would feel as though it were happening for the first time and in my mind's eye I would plot his destruction. Now, the bible says, to be angry and sin not; well, I was angry and sinning. The problem I was having was that I could not remember those events without reliving them. I knew this because of the intense emotion that I felt and the devious plots of destruction that were coming to mind. As long as my thoughts continued to focus on my bully, I was not focusing on God. The devil's plan was working like a charm until I discovered the power of forgiveness. When I began to forgive the bully of his abusiveness toward me, I was released from this stronghold. Keep in mind this was an experience to free my heart and mind as I have not physically seen him in a long, long time. As I showed love to him, I felt better because I knew that this is what God did for me.

However, the enemy's plan remained in place except instead of a childhood bully it was the teacher that did not like me or it was when my parents unjustly disciplined me or it was when my sister turned the TV off when I wanted to watch cartoons (everything is fair game); the difference was that as each *new* event came to my mind, I immediately knew how to handle it. This is when I fully

The Roots of Love

embraced the notion that the person who needs to be forgiven does not have to be in front of you to be forgiven nor do you have to talk directly to them; this is proof that forgiveness is really about the attitude of the heart. Every time I released something from my heart, I became freer. Since I now have my freedom, my past no longer holds me captive. I can remember without the pain; I can laugh without masking hurt; and I can even sit with my back to a door in a restaurant. See, my insecurity, led me to have major issues with being in a position of vulnerability, like having my back to a door, being blindfolded or even being in a pitch black room. I have come to understand that my primary responsibility is to share the love that has been given me with all those I come in contact; more importantly, it is to share with those to whom I have to seek out.

Evangelism is a product of love and was made evident through Jesus. Jesus did not come for the righteous but for the unrighteous. He came for those who needed to be loved; this is why Jesus would spend time with known thieves and prostitutes, they needed love and no one was showing them love. You can create more loyalty with forgiveness, than you can with fear and intimidation. The sinners in Jesus' time, as in today's time, were rejected and isolated. Forced to live in an unforgiving world, most likely these people felt helpless and believed that their only recourse was to continue the life they had known, but thanks be to God! Our redeemer lives! The price was paid once and for all. God continues to avail Himself to His people; this is why we received the mandate to go into the world to preach the gospel. We are extensions of God's mercy and grace that is to manifest in someone's life.

It is our responsibility to share the gospel of Jesus Christ with those who do not know Him and even to show this love with those who do know Him. It would be nice to embrace and accept every brother and sister in the church as those who know how to share the love of Christ, unfortunately, many who come to church are those who need to know the love of Christ as well. The righteous, those are who upright or in right standing with God, do not immediately walk in the fullness of God's love. In other words, just because you are saved does not mean that you know Christ; it does mean that you recognize that you no longer want to continue to live life as you have been and therefore are releasing yourself to God's care. New converts know that something has happened and appreciate the intense emotion that radiates through their body, but still have not identified with the love of God. As it relates to experiencing or embracing God's love, a new convert has taken the first step of this wonderful journey and the one who has not been converted is still searching for love (usually in all the wrong places). Jesus did not come for the righteous but for the sinner.

Jesus spent time with thieves and prostitutes because He wanted to show them the one thing they could not steal or seduce away; a thing called love. In Luke 19:1-9, Jesus saw Zacchaeus, a wealthy tax collector up in a sycamore tree. He climbed the tree because he was a man short in stature but wanted to see Jesus. Jesus called him down out of the tree and said that he must stay at his house today. After the grumbling of the people about the sinful nature of Zacchaeus and Zacchaeus' promise to return what he had stolen, Jesus said "Today salvation has come to this house . . . for the Son of Man came to seek and save the lost." Another example is when the prostitute was caught in adultery and was brought before Him; Jesus was asked what should happen to her. His defense of her came by way of one statement. Since these *righteous* men wanted to stone her, Jesus said "He who has not sinned cast the first stone." No one could throw anything and shortly thereafter Jesus forgave her of her sins. This love that Jesus showed is the same love we must show.

Now, this does not mean run out and find every wicked person to show love; it does mean to be open to share what God has done in your life with someone or anyone who may need love. Furthermore, everyone who needs love is not living in a homeless shelter; CEO's, presidents, professors,

The Roots of Love

business owners, doctors, lawyers, etc. there is no one side of town that has a monopoly on hurt but at times outward success does a great job of masking the pain. Although we were bought with a price and have been redeemed, there are those who do not know how to get to the Father's door. This is where we come in; God has shown us love and as much as it was shown to us, we must now show it to others. If God has loved you away from drugs and alcohol, then you have the ability to love someone away from drugs and alcohol through the sharing of your testimony. Your understanding of that stronghold and can help someone else receive the same gift of love from God that you received. However, you must be wise in your love sharing; getting delivered from alcohol and immediately returning to the bar for ministry is not wise. You may not be equipped to handle the temptation even if you are given a way out. Nonetheless, we have a responsibility to love our brothers and sisters because God first loved us.

This love for our brother is described perfectly in John 15:13, "Greater love has no one than this that he lay down his life for his friends." There is a misconception or limitation on this scripture that warrants a little clarification. Although it clearly fits, this scripture is not restricted to taking a bullet or jumping in front of a car to save your friend at your own peril; this scripture is not just about a physical death. Laying your life down means that your reputation or position is set aside for the sake of your friend; it means that no matter what someone else thinks of you, nor how you are negatively affected you may become, you will put your life aside to save your friend's. A few years ago, I was part of a group taking a tour out of the country. Prior to the trip I had two separate visions of a dear friend being in danger. Once, we were riding on a sky lift and the lift she was on broke; somehow she ended up hanging out of the side of the sky lift (I know this sounds like something out of a movie but it is what I saw); another time, she was stuck on the side of a cliff (I promise you I am not making this up); in both instances, I was the only

The Roots of Character

one who could get to her and had to put myself in danger in order to do so. Naturally, I dismissed this as a vivid and overactive imagination but in hindsight God was preparing me for what was to come while we were on tour. No, she was not on the side of a mountain or hanging from a sky lift (compared to what was going on those would have been easy). I know you are curious but what happened is not the point of the story. God showed me that a major and dangerous thing would happen to her and I would have to be the one to *save* her and more importantly, I had to face the danger myself in order to so. I would have to forget about my reputation, my position and my life to keep her safe and I responded appropriately.

The *event* happened early in the tour and therefore my running interference was to last about four or five days; I had to forget about myself and concentrate on her keeping her sanity in all that confusion. We were like twins during those remaining days because she could not get pass what had happened and therefore needed protection. We survived and in the end, key relationships were temporarily broken but permanently adjusted. After we returned to the states, the lingering affect of the tour remained, but was not as intense for her; it became more intense for me because I ran interference. Afterwards, I realized that the visions were from God; the same visions that I discounted as imagination had proven to be prophetic. This was extremely comforting to me because I knew beyond all doubt that I had done what I was supposed to do. In time, all wounds were healed. Not only had I received revelation of what it means to lay down your life for your friend, but God also saw me fit enough to stand up under the pressures of this ordeal (although He was the One keeping me up). This is another meaning to the expression, *tough love*. Facing the fire on someone else's behalf on the basis of a developing understanding of God is tough, but this is just what Jesus did as He maintained the integrity of love.

To maintain integrity, which is the integrity of the Word and Jesus is the Word, God has to keep all His promises.

The Roots of Love

This is supported by Numbers 23:19, "God is not a man, that He should lie, nor a son of man, that He should change His mind." This scripture relates to the promises of God and not the notion that God does not change His mind. God does change his mind, if He did not then what good were the Old Testament prophets. For example, the Prophet Isaiah told King Hezekiah to put his house in order because he was about to die; this message from God came because Hezekiah had become prideful and was taking God's glory. Hezekiah humbled himself and repented and God spared his life (See 2 Chronicles 32:24-26, Isaiah 38:1-7 and 2 Kings 20:1-4). Another example of God changing His mind is found in Exodus 32:1-14. Aaron had finished fashioning a golden calf and the Israelites had turned their backs on God. God said to Moses, "Leave me alone so my anger may burn against them and that I may destroy them." Moses interceded on their behalf and God relented and did not bring the disaster on His people. In other words God changes His mind as it relates to His wrath or judgment on the basis of repentance and intercession, but as for His promises God must adhere to His own Word. Hence, we have to maintain the integrity of not only the Word, but also our words.

    The greatest measure of one's character is the power invoked through the use of words. Words do not define character, but they can command respect; respect is a forerunner to leadership. Leadership is maximized as the leader's words are accepted; acceptance is established through the validation of spoken words. Simply, if the words of a leader can be trusted, then so can a warning. Not long ago, my sister was playing with my son and he wanted something that he should not have; rather than explaining to him why he could not have it, she merely said that "It was hot." Her intentions were good in that she knew he could not and should not have whatever he was after, but she did him a disservice by treating him as if he would not understand. As he grows, he may come to realize that she did not tell him the truth; therefore, when she does legitimately warn him about something, he may recall that moment and not listen to a bona fide warning. I know this is a stretch relative to this situation, but let me tell you how I stopped believing my parents. I was told and led to believe that there was a big, fat man in a red suit that comes once a year to bring toys to good little boys and girls; Santa Claus was his name. I believed this for maybe five years, when my siblings thought to show me *love* and tell me the truth. After I finished crying and having my mother comfort me I asked, "How am I going to get toys for Christmas?" As I began to mature, I reflected on that moment and concluded that my parents told lies; I ignored that they were supposedly doing it for my happiness and my thoughts turned to "What else are that lying about?" I stopped believing them for a season (admittedly this had a lot to do with my own seed of rebellion, but the *lie* only added fuel to fire). Occasionally, I had wondered what things would have been like if they told us that they loved us and wanted to do something special for me and my brothers and sisters. We must be careful with our words for a misguided word can have dire consequences, but a wellplaced word can bring restoration.

As a young man, in my pre-love days, I was sharp tongued and oft times brutal in my speech; I completely ignored how my words would cause someone to feel and let whomever have it with both barrels (these unfortunate actions and reactions were predicated upon my upbringing). For example, I was shown a paper that a fellow student had written; the purpose behind my seeing it was to proofread it for grammatical errors. Rather than talking one on one, I held the paper and read aloud what was written. There were several people around that added to the embarrassment that I was promoting. I knew what I was doing was causing hurt but I did not know how to show love. I did eventually help, but not until the mockery was done. I told this story to a friend of mine and explained that this student had come to me on several subsequent occasions for help. Rhetorically, I asked, "Why would someone keep coming

The Roots of Love

back, when I was verbally abusive and insulting, despite the fact that I would eventually help?" His response surprised me, he said "People want the truth and when they come to you they know that is what they will get." Even though I am being mean and insensitive? He shocked me again by saying yes. It took some time, but I learned to tell the truth with compassion.

This does not mean that I did not tell lies and that my words were always kind, it does mean that I had begun to know the difference. Lying or the lack of integrity was such a part of me it was going to take more than one revelation to cause me to overcome this. I was so accustomed to lying, that I would lie just because it was easier than telling the truth. It was like I was conditioned to lie. Thank God for deliverance! I remember once when I lied to my boss. He asked me to do something and called a few minutes to see if I had done it. On the basis of his intensity, I lied and said that I had. Another time, I was driving and hit a deer. I saw the deer on the ground writhing in pain and felt terrible. A friend asked me if I felt bad about the deer and I lied. I did feel bad, but I did not want it to be known; this was that *man thing*. As I reflect on both of these lies, I realized that I lied for the same reason; a reason that is common to all lies, fear. I did not want my friends to think that I was soft by caring about some *dumb* deer that ran in front of my car; nor did I want to be subject to my the wrath of my boss. I was not afraid of him I just did not want to be lengthy lecture on responsibility because he may have been having an off day. These experiences and many others like them taught me the importance of the telling the truth; I no longer allow anyone to cause fear to manifest itself in me. I am not afraid of anyone and do not fear the truth. I now speak because I believe. I will use wisdom, but I will tell the truth.

However, this element of integrity is greater than merely telling the truth. Integrity will place you in the position where you may have to stand alone to protect your faith. Integrity means that at times you may upset someone because you will not conform. This is not about being stubborn or rebellious; this is about discipline and determination. There was an occasion on the job where I was asked to do something that did not sit well with me; the situation was not illegal and there were no repercussions. I did not want to do it because a legitimate agreement had been made and should have been honored. Everything was explained to me concerning the events that led up to the agreement and there was a legitimate meeting of the minds. Therefore, despite a subsequent feeling of being taken advantage of, i.e., buyer's remorse, there was nothing wrong with the agreement. Getting the short end of the stick in fair negotiations is not a reason to renege on the deal. The issue for me boiled down to integrity. I was unable to influence the decision to rescind the deal (never mind that the other party had already completed their end of the contract) but was to be the one to contact the other party to inform him of the decision. Again, this was about integrity and did come easily for me. The only way to make this right would be for the other party to agree to modify the agreement although his end was complete. What is impossible with man is possible with God. God graced me with the words in a letter to communicate the post completion counter offer and it was accepted. The modified agreement suited everyone, but more importantly the integrity of my developing relationship with God was not compromised.

One of the greatest elements of God's love is that even if I had violated His Word, He would still love me. As recorded in Romans 8:38, "For I am persuaded that neither death nor life, neither angels nor demons, neither things present nor the future, nor any powers, neither height nor depth, nor anything else in all creation, will be able to separate us from the love of God that is in Christ Jesus our Lord." Love is the greatest root and can not be taken away.

The Roots of Vision

You have a vision for a successful business; one that is guaranteed to make a lot of money. You have the ability to do it and even have the support of those around you. However, you have not written it down. You have seen the signs that are in front of the shop and the new cars that will be purchased as a result of your success, but you can not go to the bank because you have not written down anything. If your only plan to be a millionaire is filling out the paper work that comes in that little gold envelope, then not only will you not become a millionaire, but you will eventually order some magazines! There was someone who had told me his vision; admittedly it was a solid idea. He was able to answer all my probing questions concerning this business venture. I was even more impressed with his market strategy. He asked me to help him with as it relates to the financial elements. I was agreeable to this, but the first thing that I asked for was his written plan. Of course, he did not have one and this was another area where he was wanted my help. I was not discouraged at this point because at least he recognized the need. The thing that did discourage me was his lack of willingness to legitimately document the vision. I could have helped him in many areas, but the one thing I can not do is tell him what the vision was that he said God had given him. I can ask questions, record and even research, but I can not establish or create a vision for someone else. He needed to be the primary participant in recording his vision and make the final decisions concerning what God had given him, but appeared to be loading me with the dominant responsibilities. I quickly concluded that what he had was a nice, dressed up dream; this was not a vision at all.

The Roots of Character

The problem was not know how in terms of documenting the vision; the problem was his lack of interest in the documentation process. I made this statement to a friend of mine and it was applicable here as well, "I can not lead you unless I know where you want to go." Unfortunately, he could never tell me and that vision was merely a nice, thick blanket draped over the future of a dreamer.

A written vision becomes a road map; not only does it tell you where you are going, but also how to get there. If your vision is not written, then when times become hard or when you see what someone else is doing, then you may lose focus and embrace the temptation to change direction. In Habakkuk 2:2-3 the bible records, "Write down the revelation and make it plain on the tablets so that a herald may run with it. For the revelation awaits an appointed time; it speaks of the end and will not prove false. Though it linger, wait for it; it will certainly come and will not delay."

In biblical context, these scriptures relate to Habakkuk's revelation that the wicked will receive their just reward by God. However, for this writing the point is also applicable, especially when you consider the great leaders in God who died still holding to their faith as recorded in Hebrews 11; for emphasis, in verse 39 and 40, the bible states, "These were all commended for their faith, yet none of them received what had been promised. God had planned something better for us so that only together with us would they be made perfect. Verse 40 brings to light another reason to write the vision, you may not live to see it come to pass; any vision that God has given me I have a responsibility to my son and all of God's people to record it such that he will be able to continue where I leave off. If it stays in the head, when the head is no longer functioning, then the vision will die.

This notion leads to a third reason to record the vision; one of the places where the greatest spiritual battles take place is in the mind. From the time you get up in the morning, the devil is attacking your mind with all kinds of

The Roots of Vision

foolishness. Even though you are still in the house, anger may come upon you because of the thoughts that come to your mind regarding someone you may have to see or something that you need to do. If you are angry and fired up before leaving the house, unless get control of your mind and thoughts, you may not have a great day because of the thoughts you entertained. See, a vision from God is not to be taken lightly and your mind needs to be clear; effectively God is putting a stamp of approval on you that says you are His and available to be used by Him to destroy the devil's work. Keeping this detailed assignment in your mind, the same place that needs to be cleaned is comparable to keeping your child in a dumpster. Visions are designed and given to change lives; not just the lives of those around today, but also of the coming generations. The reason the bible speaks of running with the vision or revelation is because runners have a specific mission and are focused on the task at hand. A herald is one who carries or proclaims an important message. Imagine running with the purpose of not only telling of the good news, but also of testifying of what God had expressly done or will do in the lives of His people. Runners have a known start and finish; when the race begins, their steps are quick and decisive but soon there is a nice stride; at this point, it does not matter what the other runners are doing because of their focus. Remember the brilliance at the Atlanta Olympics shown by Michael Johnson in the 400 meters; the comment was that "He was cruising!" If a vision is not written, then there can be no cruising.

    Have you ever described something to someone or have someone described something to you and the response or thought is *stop dreaming*? Would the response have been the same if it were spelled out in detail on paper? The brother I mentioned earlier, with the great business idea, has had several subsequent visions from God; those too have gone unfulfilled. It is difficult to tell someone that their life changing vision is a glorified dream. God will not continue to expand your vision if you have not accomplished

The Roots of Character

the first part of the original assignment. A vision is like a talent and it will be taken away if not used. Paraphrased, Luke 16:10 states, if you demonstrate faithfulness over little that you have, then you are showing the character traits to be able to handle more. If God has given you a vision for a successful business and you have not done anything with it, He would not turn around and give you another vision. Likewise, if your vision continues to change direction from month to month, week to week or day to day and nothing is being accomplished, then you may want to check with God to verify the vision He gave you. You may be mixing in your wants with God's plans; God will not expand your borders or reward you for walking outside of His plans and purposes. Staying with God's plans requires discipline.

Discipline is a prerequisite to focus; focus allows you to appreciate that God's purpose for your life may not be the same as someone else's. Therefore, you do not have to imitate the activities of someone beyond imitating their faith. Simply, if two persons believe God for a house, one can receive a 3,000 square foot house and the other may receive a small town home; the latter does not have to envy or feel discontentment toward the larger homeowner because God gives in accordance to what we can handle. If the owner of the townhouse sells the home for a larger one on the basis of envy or jealousy, then this person may never have peace in that home; remember the blessings of God are without reproach. Also, this is an area where humility must prevail. Just because someone else has it and it looks nice does not mean that it is for you, even if you are older and have been established longer. God knows the plans that he has for you and if you try to force God's hand, you will only hurt yourself. When the bible says, "... unless we become as little children," it is not intended to mean that we should act like children and have to have what the other kid has.

In Proverbs 29:18 the bible states "Where there is no revelation, the people cast off restraint." In other words,

The Roots of Vision

they have no focus and are subject to change directions with the wind. The magnitude of vision, the written vision, is directly linked to success in God. Once documented, a vision eliminates deniability or a failing memory. There is a constant reminder of what the vision is and how to achieve the desired end. The difference between a vision and a dream is whether or not it is documented. Martin Luther King is renowned for his *I have a dream* speech, but in reality he was sharing his vision. Dreams are what people do when they are asleep or not paying attention to their immediate surroundings. Dreams are elements that have impacted your subconscious that are reproduced in some unknown sequence while sleeping. Notwithstanding, God does communicate through dreams, but these messages from God give direction and bring clarity; they are not the dreams that I am referring. The dreams that I am referring to are comparable to fantasies. A fantasy is an imagined event or condition fulfilling a wish. To clarify, a fantasy is the unwritten business idea that is going to make millions of dollars; this is a product of your imagination and only serves to make you appear to be extremely foolish. The bible records in Proverbs 12:11b, "He who chases fantasies lacks judgment."

On the other hand, visions are created or established while conscious; they are often the product of deliberate meditation on a particular subject matter deposited in your spirit by God. A written vision allows you to see clearly at all times and should provide the details to accomplish the assignment. This does not mean once the vision is written that you are guaranteed success, but it does mean that if it is not written, then there is almost a guarantee of failure. In this regard, a vision is a stated goal. This goal should stretch you or challenge you to apply your faith in certain areas; otherwise it is not a goal. For example, when God took my rib, he fashioned my wife; I love her tremendously but I do not have the goal to be a good husband; likewise, my sons add to my heaven on earth experience and continue to teach me so much about life, but I do not have the goal to be a good father. I can be a good husband and completely satisfy my wife but if I am ignoring my sons in the process, then I am failing; I can be a good father and totally enjoy and embrace the development of my sons, but not at the expense of my wife. I can be a good husband and father thereby, satisfying my immediate family, but it could cost me my parents, siblings, friends, or anyone else who may need or want from me. As such my goal or vision has to be broader; hence my vision is to be a good man. As a good man I can legitimately satisfy the demands placed on me; this is done with balance and understanding, but does challenge me to maximize my growth and development in God since He is the One who sustains me.

In summary, perhaps the greatest responsibility you have to a God given vision is to write it down; I explained earlier about the continuation of the vision should you not see it within your lifetime, but there is another purpose to it as well. This relates to your ability to grow and develop in God and to establish a clear pattern of God's communication. A vision from God is a prophecy; prophecies tell of things that have not come to pass, but usually carry an assurance from God that it will come to pass. As your prophecy is documented, you will have recorded a message from God about some future activity or personal miracle. Once it happens (record that also) you now have proof of God's relationship and communication with you and more importantly you can testify to your children, friends, spouse, church, everyone about what God promised you by way of the vision and the subsequent fulfillment of that promise. This testimony will not only encourage others in the faith, but it will elevate your faith in God. You may be propelled to study and read the Word even more because He used you to complete His work! There is nothing more frustrating or discouraging than forgetting what God has said concerning your life. After it comes to pass and God has done what He said He will do, you should be able to provide documentation of God's promise; not for someone else, but for your own sake. The more you write down, the more you will have to hold on to when things appear to be contrary to God's promise. There is no greater encouragement than the recorded Word of God.

The Roots of a Renewed Mind

By definition, did you know that faith and fear are the same? Faith believes that something that has not happened will happen. Fear believes that something that has not happened will happen. However, there is a difference in the application or use of these; that difference is based on how you see. For example, I know of a few people who are deathly afraid of flying. Actually, it is an abrupt landing that is at the core of this fear. Fear drives the actions of these persons. They are limited by the notion that the plane will have some mechanical problems and come crashing to the ground. They could just as easily believe that the plane would not have any problems and will take them safely to the intended destination. One is fear and the other is faith; one allows you to live freely and the other keeps you in bondage. Depending on the call of God on someone, say to the mission field, then God's plan for this person is temporarily being hindered by this fear. Fear causes you to doubt and reject God and is the product of an unchanged mind.

Before I learned to swim, I recall being at the pool with a few guys from the neighborhood; of course, they could swim. They explained to me how easy it was to swim, specifically, they told me that if I jumped in, I would go to the bottom and would be able to push off the bottom and quickly come back to the top. They even demonstrated how this worked; by the way, the water was eleven feet deep. Fear was all over me, but I became convinced by their words and example. I stood on the edge and jumped; everything was working fine until I hit the water. We had talked about every facet of this process except for one thing, what if I did not make it to the bottom. I did not go

The Roots of a Renewed Mind

to the bottom because I did not jump in properly. One of the guys came in after me, of course by this time I was in full panic mode; so when I felt someone near me, I grabbed on. I was climbing on him so hard and with such force, he had to let me go or he would have drowned. The other guy who was there grabbed my hand and put it on the side railing; I think my fingerprints may still be in the metal. I was in such panic, with my hands flapping all over, that I never realized I was at the top of the water. I vowed never to do that again and immediately fear had taken up resident in my heart concerning swimming. There was nothing that was going to make me get back in the water; nothing except my desire to overcome this fear. As I entered high school, it was a requirement to take swimming and therefore I had to do what I said I would not do, get back in the water. I quickly discovered that my problem was not that I could not swim, but that I was letting the fear control my actions. I practiced in the shallow end of the pool; I learned how to breathe, but more importantly how to control my anxiety. As the year went on, I became more and more comfortable and wanted to test these skills in the deep water. Without telling anyone and seemingly with no one looking, I went to the deep in of the pool, climbed on the small diving board and jumped in; I swam to the edge and the celebration began. That monkey was off my back! I did not stop there, I climbed back up there again, but this time I made sure I had everyone's attention (the whole class, including the teacher new my story) and jumped in again and swam to the edge. That monkey was now dead!

    I overcame my fear of the water by working on my mind. I legitimately learned the mechanics to swimming instead of just listening to someone else's experience. I came to understand that the water was not the enemy, but I was my own enemy because of what I chose to believe. I stopped feeding myself negative information and began to transform my mind. In the end, the advice that my friends had given me was true, but I learned this through experience. I wish I knew God during those years but in hindsight, I know I had learned the meaning to God's Word as found in 2 Timothy 1:7, "For God did not give us a spirit of fear, but a spirit of power, of love and a sound mind." After this experience, my mind was renewed as it relates to the water, but it would be years later before I would begin the process of renewal for God. Nevertheless, I knew that the principles I had learned could be universally applied and by taking the time to develop, all fear can eliminated. I realized that fear is a byproduct of not knowing and that the true reason people fear the unknown is that they know so much about themselves. Fear, if allowed, can raise its head even among God's great.

Elijah was a great servant of God but was led astray by fear. By way of background (for complete detail read 1 Kings 17-19), Elijah spoke the words, "There will be neither dew nor rain in the next few years except at my word" and God honored these words spoken through Elijah. Elijah was feed by a raven; a raven is a scavenger who eats on dead carcasses. Since God's Word had already gone forth about eating *blood* this raven had to bring Elijah cooked food. Elijah had been used to perform miracles, including resurrecting a widow's son and calling fire down from heaven to kill false prophets. After all this, Elijah allowed fear to enter in his heart and ran from Jezebel because she threatened his life. 1 Kings 19:3 states, "Elijah was afraid and ran for his life." Elijah, at the leading of the Angel of the Lord, made his way to the mountain of God where he spent the night in a cave. Then in verses 9b and 13b, God asked this question, "What are you doing here Elijah?" In other words, how could you fear this woman after all I have done through you? Have you lost your mind?

Elijah thought that he was the only one remaining that was loyal to God since all the other prophets had been killed. God told him that he had seven thousand more and that he was not the only one; afterwards God told Elijah to anoint Elisha as his successor. Fear caused Elijah to lose his position in God; Elijah's only remaining task was to prepare Elisha for the work of the Lord. If you do not overcome the elements of fear that may be working against you in your life, God will replace you. Elijah had done many great things for God and in His name, but was not renewed in his mind. Elijah's fear undermined the glory of God. Someone with the ability to cause God to act and demonstrate His power was running in fear; effectively, Elijah actions indicated that he feared Jezebel more than God. Fear causes you to act contrary to God's word, even if it is only disbelief. This is why our minds must be renewed; renewal is the only way to maximize what God wants to do in your life.

Earlier I told you of my mother and the special bond we have; we share a closeness that is beyond measure. However, my relationship with my father was almost the opposite and yet through his process of renewal I am encouraged daily in the awesomeness of God. My father was always a pillar of strength and clearly the man of the house. He placed a great emphasis on working and was committed to providing for his family; these ethics, I would later learn were inherited from his father. He had a commanding presence that was always felt. He was not perfect nor without fault; we experienced some difficult times growing up and most of the time I learned to blame my father for them. It was not until later, much later, that I could appreciate my father for his efforts. The mistakes were there, but I could not sit in judgment of him; I had come to understand that my father did the best that he could for us and for that I am grateful.

As it relates to his renewal, my father went from drinking to being drunk in the Holy Spirit. He went from daily readings about John Riggins (former running back for the Washington Redskins) to reading about John the Baptist. He went from midnight partying to midnight prayer meetings; from bad decision making to being a disciple; my father has been renewed. It is written in 2 Corinthians 5:17, "If anyone is in Christ, he is a new creation; the old has gone, the new has come." My father's experience in God to this point testifies about renewal. I am proud of

The Roots of Character

the growth and development in him concerning the things of God. Although I never asked him how he renewed his mind, but am most certainly assured it was his choice. I never asked how the transformation began, but may have found the answer in the Book of Deuteronomy.

In Deuteronomy 32:23-29 the bible records, "I will heap calamities upon them and spend my arrows against them. I will send wasting famine against them, consuming pestilence and deadly plague; I will send against them the fangs of the beasts, the venom of vipers that glide in the dust. In the street the sword will make them childless; in their homes terror will reign. Young men and women will perish infants and gray haired men. I said I would scatter them and blot out their memory from mankind, but I dreaded the taunt of the enemy, lest the adversary misunderstand and say, 'Our hand had triumphed; the Lord has not done all this.' They are a nation without sense; there is no discernment in them. If only they were wise and would understand this and discern what their end will be!" These verses are part of the Song of Moses that he recited from beginning to end to the Israelites. Through idol worship and sacrifice to demons, the Israelites had turned their backs on God. Moses was explaining what would happen to all those who continue to ignore God. Actually, he was hoping to encourage the Israelites to respond to God with the honor and reverence due Him and to begin to live holy lives in accordance with His instructions. In verse 35, God says, "It is mine to avenge and I will repay. In due time their foot will slip; their day of disaster is near and their doom rushes upon them." I refer to Deuteronomy, i.e., *do-you-run-to-me* as the Book of Choices, for God is giving us the opportunity to chose Him over certain destruction.

In demonstration of His love, God actually is a God of second chances (sometimes). The Israelites were not always obedient to God and needed encouragement to turn back to God. This is what the Lord says to the Israelites in Amos 4:6-11, "I gave you empty stomachs in every city and lack of bread in every town, yet you have not returned

The Roots of a Renewed Mind

to me," declares the Lord. "I also withheld rain from you when the harvest was still three months away. I sent rain to one town, but withheld it from another. One field had rain; another had none and dried up. People staggered from town to town for water, but did not have enough to drink, yet you have not returned to me," declares the Lord. "Many times I struck your gardens and vineyards; I struck them with blight and mildew. Locusts devoured your fig and olive trees, yet you have not returned to me," declares the Lord. "I sent plagues among you as I did to Egypt. I killed your young men with the sword, along with your captured horses. I filled your nostrils with the stench of your camps, yet you have not returned to me," declares the Lord. "I overthrew some of you as I overthrew Sodom and Gomorrah. You were like a burning stick snatched from the fire, yet you have not returned to me," declares the Lord. Through God's love, sometimes tough love, the Israelites eventually turned toward God and were restored.

My father was not an Israelite, but had his own choices to make and made the right choice; he is now and avid student of the Word and an encouragement too many. As for me, I followed in his footsteps and also serve God. I too had my share of failures and gross mistakes, but was converted; conversion being the renewal of the mind to conform to the Spirit of Christ. Since I have been converted, I am no longer a sinner and therefore my past sins can not be used against me; anyone who knew me then only knew a shadow of who I am. This is to say that when I am reminded of what I used to do or what I used to say, I can stay focused and not become defensive. A renewed mind liberates you from the past. My transformation was as simple as the ABCs: I can boldly say that where there used to be apathy, there is now appreciation; I may have been bad, but now I am born again; contempt was replaced by confession. I used to be dangerous, but I have been delivered. I have gone from excuses to exaltation; from foolishness to faith; from greed to grace and goodness. I moved from hatred to hallelujah; from insolence to integrity; from jealousy to Jesus. I changed from killing, to Kingdom; from lust, to love; from mean to meditation; from nothing to nourishing. I discovered that I did not have to be obstinate, so I chose obedience; pride was overcome by praise; quarrelsome was removed by quietness; my reproach fell victim to repentance and sin was redeemed by my Savior. All of my troubles have turn to testimonies. I went from unholy to united; from violence to victory and from wretched to worship. I went from a being X rated to being X-cited about God; once I was yoked and now I am youthful; I was renewed from being a master zinger to being zealous for Jesus. These ABCs are *about becoming Christlike.*

As it relates to choices and the renewal process, I am reminded of a dream that I had. I was raking my yard when I noticed a small, brown snake with black markings. It could not have been more than a couple of inches long; not big enough to be concerned with and therefore I let my curiosity lead me. With the rake, I picked up the snake for a slightly closer look; the snake began to move about and fell to the ground. Again, I picked up the snake, but it appeared to be a little larger than what I originally saw; again it slithered around and fell to the ground; I was really curious at this point and picked the snake up third time. This time it was big and as it moved across the rake it quickly turned toward me and I jumped back! Fortunately, at this point I woke up; I did not want to pick that snake up again. I prayed about this dream because I know what snakes represent and wanted to know what this dream meant. The answer was pretty obvious, stop playing with snakes, they will turn on you; in other words, the devil is not something to be curious about and therefore stay focused on the work before you. At the time that I had this dream, I was in the middle of renewing my mind and there were some things that I had not let go of yet; this dream was an eye opener to let go of anything that was not godly and to focus completely on the things of God.

The Roots of a Renewed Mind

That dream was a message to not allow the truth about God to be suppressed; to not allow foolish things to stay in my mind, but allow myself to be fully transformed. In Romans 1:24-26, the Word of God says that ". . . God gave them over in the sinful desires of their hearts to sexual impurity for the degrading of their bodies with one another. They exchanged the truth of God for a lie, and worshiped and served created things rather than the Creator, who is praised forever. Because of this God gave them over to shameful lusts. In verse 28, "Furthermore, since they did not think it worthwhile to retain the knowledge of God, He gave them over to a depraved mind; to do what ought not to be done." I will never forget that dream, but more importantly I will never forget God's warning through the dream.

The Roots of Giving

To truly understand giving you must examine how Jesus handled money; unfortunately, the one who handled Jesus' money was the same one who betrayed him. Surely, the question of where we would be without Jesus has come across our minds or has been said in conversation; additionally, I have also wondered, what if it were not Judas who betrayed Jesus. Most likely, there would have been a *Book of Judas*. This book would detail how Jesus would have spent money and provided the greatest foundation of stewardship, reciprocity and giving than any other resource. Nonetheless, no where in the bible does it state that Jesus was financially or materially rich; it is recorded in 2 Corinthians 8:9 that "The grace of our Lord Jesus Christ, that though He was rich, yet for your sakes He became poor, so that you through his poverty might become rich." The riches that Jesus gave up were the riches of being in the presence of and constantly communing with God; this is where the true riches are and only through Jesus can we ever obtain true riches. Since Jesus was not financially or materially rich, but was blessed through his ministry, how he used money was a major concern to not only Judas, but to the other disciples as well. The bible says in Matthew 26:6-9, "A woman came to Him with an alabaster jar of very expensive perfume, which she poured on His head as He was reclining at the table. When the disciples (notice the *s* on disciple) saw this, they (more than one) were indignant. "Why this waste?" They (more than one) asked. "This perfume could have been sold at a high price and the money given to the poor." In John 12:2-11, the above scenario is described except that the statements made were attributed to Judas. John is

The Roots of Giving

correct in that these statements were made by Judas, but also the other disciples accepted Judas' words and became incensed. What the other disciples did not know was the motive behind Judas Iscariot's objections.

Judas used to steal from Jesus; in verse 6 of John 12, the bible says "He (Judas) did not say this because he cared about the poor but because he was a thief; as keeper of the money bag, he used to help himself to what was put into it." Jesus put a thief in charge of the money! Since Judas was already stealing from God, this made it easier for the devil to encourage him to betray Jesus. This is evidence of the notion that there is no such this as a little sin; all sin creates gateways or paths to other sin. As such, the devil did not have to search for someone to betray Jesus; Judas Iscariot, through his thievery, effectively volunteered to become Satan's ally in killing Jesus.

Not only was Judas stealing money from Jesus, but his betrayal was for money. The taste for sin, in this instance the love of money, will cause you to hunger more for it; ultimately it becomes a stronghold and then all restraint is cast aside in your pursuit of this thing that you seemingly must have. This stronghold for Judas leads him to identify Jesus to the soldiers for 30 pieces of silver coins. Now, the same devil that entered Judas and encouraged his betrayal is the same devil that magnified the guilt and remorse of Judas to the point of suicide. Judas hung himself (Matthew 27:5), but it did not end there for Judas; as found in Acts 1:18, "With the reward he got for his wickedness, Judas bought a field; there he fell headlong (this is after the hanging), his body burst open and all his intestines spilled out." As the ravens or crows fed on his flesh of his natural body, his spirit man went to hell.

Judas had the most trusted position and failed in his stewardship; this thief could not appreciate giving money away. A thief may not understand the spiritual investments Jesus was making through the feeding of the poor; a thief may not comprehend that one of the greatest things someone can do for another is to give them something without expectation of return; nor can a thief embrace the principle of Love. In case you are wondering, a thief is not just someone who takes from another, but also withholds the blessings of God that have manifested in their lives. This not only includes tithes and offerings but also love, kindness, compassion, forgiveness, etc.; basically anything that has been given to you that is not shared is equivalent to stealing God's glory. Like it was with Judas, so it may be with many, as such, we all need to be reminded that we can not serve two masters.

The bible says in Matthew 6:24b, that "You can not serve both God and money." One of the ways to overcome money is to recognize money for what it is. First, money is a tool. God gives us the power or ability to get wealth in order to confirm His covenant with our forefathers; the purpose of this wealth is to further the work of the kingdom. Ministries cost money and only through the prospering of God's people will His purpose be carried out for the rest of His people. Second, money is a test. Arguably, the money test is the test that is failed the most by children of God. If you want to know where someone is or if there is any doubt about someone's character, allow money to enter into your interaction. The moment money is involved everything changes; what used to be fun is now a chore because someone has ten dollars on the line (it does not matter how much money it is). However, money is also a test because it shows how responsible someone is or is not. Luke 16:10 says, "Whoever can be trusted with very little can also be trusted with much, and whoever is dishonest with very little will also be dishonest with much." The reason this test is failed so often is because there may be a lack of acceptance about God's ability to reproduce wealth. The greatest giving is not when you give to someone who can give back, but rather when you give to someone who can not. With this type of giving, you are imitating God because there is no way we can give more than what God gave us through His Son. We do not have the ability to pay God back for saving our souls; the best we can do is

The Roots of Giving

to take care of God's people while simultaneously become good stewards. Third, money is the answer. Ecclesiastes 10:19 says, "A feast is made for laughter, and wine makes life merry, but money is the answer for everything." This scripture relates to giving; normally, people do not have feasts for themselves, but it is usually connected with a gathering or celebration; generally, most people would fellowship as they are drinking wine; money answers everything because with money you can have a feast, buy wine, clothe the naked, feed the poor, build a church, etc. Money, in itself, is not the answer for everything since money can buy sex, but not love; it can buy entertainment, but not give you joy; it can make your popular, but not get establish friendships. Understand this, money answers everything as long as it is given; this is not to say that all your money should be given away as this would not be good stewardship; it is to say that if you should be open to sharing the blessings of God so that someone else may receive their blessings. To summarize, money it is a tool, a test and the answer. When you have your answer by way of money or riches, the question then becomes, "Will you continue to pass the money test and master the use of this powerful tool?"

Nonetheless, it is not enough to understand the purpose of money, but through the proper use of it you should be able to reap the benefits. There was a rich young man who asked "What must he do to get eternal life." Jesus in Matthew 19:18-19 replied, "Do not murder, do not commit adultery, do not steal, do not give false testimony, honor your father and mother, and love your neighbor as yourself." The man said that he did all that and wanted to know what he lacked. Jesus then told him, verse 21, "If you want to be perfect, go, sell your possessions and give to the poor, and you will have treasure in heaven." The rich young man sadly walked away because he had great wealth. He was an example of someone who chose money over serving God. The man's heart was in the right place because he wanted to do right by God, but his money was keeping him from serving

The Roots of Character

properly. See, he thought that the greatest thing he had was money, he failed to understand that his greatest gift was his heart for God. In modern day times this would be comparable to a pastor asking for an offering and the people begin making accusations that all the pastor wants is money and therefore will not give.

Jesus goes on to say in Matthew 19:23, "I tell you truth, it is hard for a rich man to enter the kingdom of heaven. Again I tell you, it is easier for a camel to go through the eye of a needle than for a rich man to enter the Kingdom of God." I was in conversation with someone who appeared to be a seasoned Christian. The statement made was "There is no way a camel can pass through a little needle." She did not realize that the needle was referring to the gates to the city that were like needles, since the only way in was to pass through these holes. It is difficult for a camel to lower its hump and still walk. Nonetheless, the rich young man played by all the rules, but that was not enough to receive the benefits of God that are linked to giving. Simply put, you can get God without the experience, but God can not get you without the experience. This means that you can apply God's principles and have success, but unless you submit, God does not have you. The rich man believed that all that he had was all there was; this is why he sadly walked away at Jesus' statements. He did not understand the purpose of money and besides, his money is not what Jesus was after; He was after his heart. If your heart is right, then you are positioned to be a giver to the Lord.

Although God loves a cheerful giver, I am not going to tell you to be cheerful by showing big a smile or doing back flips as giving is presented to you; walking around as if you are being tickled or shouting from the roof tops is not an indicator of cheerfulness, anymore than sitting quietly is reflective of being solemn or sad. For example, you may be ready to write God a check for a million dollars and you are so overcome that you sit quietly; at a glance you would appear not to be happy, but inside (where it matters most) you are full of unspeakable joy. Giving is personal

The Roots of Giving

and is predicated on how you feel about God. The widow who gave her last mites in an offering was not running with excitement; most likely, she had come to a place where Jesus was who she wanted and was willing to sacrifice all she had to get Him. When Jesus looked at her and held her out as an example, He was looking into her spirit and not whether or not she whooped and hollered during the offering. Since giving is more of a spiritual act as oppose to a physical one, giving should also be done in secret. To sacrificially give and then to tell that you have done so, is to received your reward in full from man. God is not pleased with your giving despite the fact that people may have benefited. In Matthew 3:3 Jesus makes this point, "Do not let your left hand know what the right hand is doing, so that your giving may be done in secret. Then your Father, who sees what is done in secret, will reward you." This private giving communicates to God that you are His and that you trust Him to meet your needs as you meet the needs of others.

This kind of giving is at the core of discipleship and is indicative of the character of Christ. Even the most casual observer would recognize that there is something different about the private giver. A quiet, unspoken confidence about the assurances of God permeates the entire being of this person. The recognized difference creates a basis of attraction because people generally will want what you have. This attraction should be lasting, since it is based on an apparent understanding of the principles of giving demonstrated by God in the giving of His Son. At the root of this great gift was the opportunity to be redeemed. It is an opportunity because a closed heart can not receive this gift; everyone has a choice to make about their relationship with God but even if you chose God, you are not guaranteed character fulfillment or the Kingdom of God. In Matthew 7:21 Jesus states, "Not everyone who says to me 'Lord, Lord,' will enter the Kingdom of Heaven, but only he who does the will of my Father who is in heaven."

God is not looking for followers of certain principles, but those who seek to apply all God's principles and precepts.

This is the derived meaning when Jesus says in Matthew 5:3, "Blessed are the poor in spirit, for theirs is the Kingdom of Heaven." Those who are poor in spirit sense the need of God in their lives and become *beggars*. Verse 4, "Blessed are those who mourn for they will be comforted." Mourning is the regret or grief over your sins. Verse 5, "Blessed are the meek, for they will inherit the earth. Not the fearful or timid, but those who completely submit to God. Verse 6, "Blessed are those who hunger and thirst for righteousness, for they will be filled." It is better to eat several small meals and digest appropriately, than to eat a big meal and not be able to do anything but sleep. Verse 7, "Blessed are the merciful for they will be shown mercy." This means to do unto others as God has done unto you. Verse 8, "Blessed are the pure in heart, for they will see God." A pure heart is based on intention and desire; it does not mean that you are without sin, but merely that your heart is right. Verse 9, "Blessed are the peacemakers for they will be called sons of God." For those who take the initiative and are on a mission from God to spread the good news of the gospel, they will be sons of God. These principles are yours to have, if your heart is open to receive.

Understand that Jesus is the fullness of the Spirit and we as human beings have a measure of the Spirit. This is why it takes all of us coming together to reflect the wholeness of Christ. Individually, our portion is not enough; as we share and reproduce after our selves then God can be glorified. We were given this opportunity and in the spirit of what we were given I issue this challenge: I dare you to apply the Word of God to your life. I dare you to pray without ceasing as found in Ephesians 6:18. James 1:6 says, "All things are possible to them that believe;" I dare you to believe. I dare you to understand that you are more than a conqueror as stated in Romans 8:28. I dare you to trust Him. I dare you to keep His Word, to

The Roots of Giving

make a stand. I dare you to ignore your age. David writes in Psalms 37:25, "I was young and am old, never have I seen the righteous forsaken or any seed begging bread." I dare you to forgive, to love, to renew your mind. I dare you to maintain the integrity of Christ. I dare you to build your character for God!

The Roots of Faith and Wisdom

At a glance, it may appear as if faith and wisdom are polar opposites or perhaps at minimum, distant cousins. In reality faith and wisdom are twins; this means that the connection between the two is so great that to speak of one, you have to consider the other. Hence, this dynamic duo is discussed together. However, allow me to dispel a few myths that seem to be coming more rapid as it relates to faith.

First, there is no blueprint on faith. Living in an area where you have to apply faith just to survive does not mean that your faith is better than the person who grew up in a comfortable environment. It is true that the application of faith through prayer may be greater, but faith itself is not. Poverty and lack are not prerequisites for touching the heart of God; it is possible to develop a deep, intense relationship with God and have wealth at the same time.

Second, there is this thing called big faith. Admittedly, I am still not sure what big faith is; I do know that Jesus said that we only needed faith the size of a grain of mustard seed and we could move mountains. However, I think the confusion may come from Jesus' statement to the Centurion's servant concerning not having found such great faith even in Israel. The Centurion, to this point, had only heard of Jesus, but he knew and experienced authority. The Centurion's faith was based on his understanding of authority; therefore he applied his understanding to his need and the result was directed faith. The wisdom of his experience afforded him the opportunity to aim his faith and allow Jesus to heal his servant. In today's time, you hear people speak of great faith and how they can believe

The Roots of Faith and Wisdom

God for anything; these statements may be true, but they are based on the experiences of the person and not some super level of faith. Even the gift of faith is rooted in the experience of having believed God for some impossibility. It only takes the faith the size of a mustard seed.

The third myth relates to *doubt*. Doubt is stating that something is not going to or did not happen; doubt is not questioning the reality of an unbelievable event, like "Is God really going to do this?" Doubt does not mean that you do not question, it means that you are not sure because a certain experience is new. Certainly, when speaking of doubt, you have to discuss the disciple referred to as *Doubting Thomas*. Thomas was a disciple of Christ who was not there when Jesus had shown himself to the other disciples after the resurrection. Thomas was told that Jesus had resurrected, but vowed not to believe until he had proof. It is for this that he is labeled as doubting Thomas. However, what is often overlooked is that after Jesus had proven to Thomas that He had resurrected, Thomas committed himself totally to the ministry of Jesus. No one could ever shake Thomas' faith because he had seen Jesus with his own eyes. Today, no one should be able shake your faith because of your experience with Jesus in your life; and yet, it still takes more than faith to truly serve God.

Dare I say, faith alone is not enough, and that it takes more than faith to do anything! James 2:26 says that "faith without works is dead." Hebrews 6:12 reads, "We do not want you to become lazy but to imitate those who through faith and patience inherit what has been promised." In these verses, faith is combined with works and patience, respectively, thereby proving that faith needs help. Also, I am aware of Hebrews 10:38 which reads "The just shall live by faith." What I am suggesting is not in contrast to this scripture, but rather an expansion of it. Invariably, we all live by faith since there is nothing within our control; we have the illusion of control and just like an oasis in the desert it disappears upon a closer look.

The Roots of Character

It is true that we should live and walk by faith; however, we should step by wisdom.

For example, suppose you are in a position to where you have to cross a frozen lake; it is imperative that you get to your destination immediately and therefore you are without choice, you must cross this pond. A partially covered sign catches your eye and as you brush away the covering to read it you see these words: *Danger, Thin Ice.* Still without options and by faith, you begin to cross the ice. You take a step and the ice cracks, so you step back. You step in another direction and you do not hear anything therefore you keep going. Another step and then a third, but on the fourth step you hear another crack and alter your steps again. You are walking by faith, but stepping by wisdom. Your whole body is tied in to your faith; every atom in you is participating in this faith walk; your eyes are looking for deep white color in the ice and your ears are listening for the cracks. At some point, you may begin to think you can not make it across and look behind you only to discover just how far you have come. There is nothing to gain by turning back. You even discover that a faith walk includes the application of your experiences and utilizes all your senses. There was more involved than just your faith.

The bible says that it is impossible to please God without faith; this is undeniably true, but without wisdom it is impossible to keep pleasing God. Using wisdom and faith together produces *applied faith.* Applied faith is focusing your faith in areas beyond your influence. God has given us the ability to do some things for ourselves and therefore we do not have to pray about doing them; we just do it. For example, if you are driving your car down a steep hill and want to keep the car from going to fast, you apply pressure to the brakes. You do not pray in Jesus' name "Lord let this car go slowly down this hill." You have the ability to hit the brakes and therefore this is not an area where you need to apply faith. If the brakes were not

The Roots of Faith and Wisdom

working, then call on Jesus to stop the car! The premise is this, we do not have to believe God for something that we are capable of doing ourselves. Faith and wisdom working together afford us the opportunity to not repeat the same mistakes.

Faith and Wisdom in Planning

There are four major points to explore in relation to combining faith and wisdom. The first is faith and wisdom in planning. Planning relates to vision and as previously discussed one of the great fallacies in our lives is a failure to write the vision down so that it becomes a map to guide you; a subsequent activity to the documentation is the planning or execution of the vision. This is to say that you can not write down the vision to be a millionaire and it automatically happens. There needs to be a plan; a plan that charts a course of action and predetermined steps that should only be altered by God. Proverbs 19:21 says, "Many are the plans of man, but the plans of God shall prevail." God's plan supercedes our plans, but that does not preclude us from planning. It only means that our minds are finite and therefore we only see in part, but God who sees and knows all overrides our limitations to maximize the blessings in our lives. As stated in Jeremiah 29:11, "For I know the plans I have for you, declares the Lord, plans to prosper you and not to harm you, plans to give you hope and a future." Our plans allow us to become rich, but God plans produce wealth. Simply put, faith says act and wisdom says plan.

A vision is a God inspired plan, but if you do not think about and consider what it takes to accomplish it, then it means nothing. Luke 14:28-30 says it this way, "Suppose one of you wants to build a tower. Will he not first sit down and estimate the cost to see if he has enough money to complete it? For if he lays a foundation and is not able to finish it, everyone who sees it will ridicule him, saying 'This fellow began to build and was not able to finish.'" To

The Roots of Character

start a project for God, knowing that He has it all, and not be able to complete it is perhaps the saddest thing in a Christian's walk. This is because all you would have to do is plan out the elements of the vision that God has given and remain open to the Holy Spirit to lead in the right path; a failure to do this preempts God's plan as it relates to the individual. Overall, God's plan will manifest itself. Planning allows you to participate in the acts of God; this does not mean you help God, rather it means that you would have maximized your thoughts, gifts and talents. Therefore, you realize that you need God to do what needs to be done because what you have come up with is not enough. In other words, planning demonstrates a faithfulness over the little that has been shown or given that will prepare you to receive more.

For example, suppose you have five dollars and need to feed your family of five; this is all the money you have and there is no other way to get money (in the absence of divine intervention). It would not be wise to go to say, McDonald's and order a Big Mac that will be cut into five pieces. The only thing that this demonstrates is lack of wisdom. However, by using a little wisdom and being faithful over those five dollars you can gain favor with God. If you bought, say, a bag of rice, vegetables and chicken stock, then you could feed your family and perhaps even have leftovers. Wisdom will get you what you need until faith produces what you want (as long as what you want is not contrary to God). Another example of faith and wisdom in planning comes from the story of a wise woman who fed her children a lot of oatmeal; she did not have much money and knew that whatever she fed the children would have to last since she knew that it would be late in the day or perhaps even the next day before they could eat again. Somehow, through the feeding of the oatmeal, the children were sustained; later in the day they could drink some water and somehow that oatmeal was still there and would give the appearance that they had a meal. The mother used wisdom and faith to preserve her family. Foresight in planning was used

The Roots of Faith and Wisdom

until God changed the situation; she used her talents and abilities to come up with a way to provide for her family, but it was God who sustained them.

Faith and wisdom in planning allowed another family to be saved. The widow at Zarephath, as recorded in 1 Kings 17:1-15, had planned to make one last meal for her and her son when Elijah had come by and requested food. However, this was the final piece to her systematic plan for life; the woman was not planning on dying nor was she interested in suicide. All the while she was praying and believing God to provide a way such that she and her son may live; upon reaching the end of oil and flour, she lost hope and believed that death was imminent for her family. She did not just run out of oil and flour, but she effectively ran out of hope and faith. The lapse of her faith does not overshadow her plan for life; she had done all she could and now it was time for God to answer her prayers or she and her son were going to die. This is why God said to Elijah in verse 9, "Go at once to Zarephath of Sidon and stay there. I have commanded a widow in that place to supply you with food." Notice that God says to *go at once,* as in, leave right now because the time has come for me to answer this woman's prayer and also that He has commanded a widow to supply him with food. Since God had given this command then she had to be talking to God about her situation that resulted in this test of faith. She knew a prophet of God was coming, but she did not know when and her faith had begun to wane. After Elijah told her to make bread for him and then for her family, he told her that the flour would not be used up and the oil would not run dry; in other words, he confirmed the word of the Lord to her and therefore she could go and make bread for him. Again I say, in contrast to her words, her plan was not to die, but to ration what she had until God provided a way out.

Planning is the practical use of the talents and abilities given. Unfortunately, there is an over dependency that we place on God. I fully recognize that God is our source and provider and it is He who makes everything possible.

The Roots of Character

However, God also has given us talents for a reason; He wants us to use them. Why should God part the waters, when you are standing next to a bridge? The idea is that we should do what we can and believe for that which is beyond our control. God gave the talent to build bridges and therefore He does not have to continue to part waters.

There are talents and abilities within all of us that we must use to glorify God. God is not happy if you keep repeating the same mistakes, thereby requiring Him to continue to deliver you from the same thing every week. Imagine if God had to keep saving you over and over again. He saves you and you revert; He delivers you and you go back; time and time again. This is what the Israelites kept doing in the book of Judges. They were enslaved and cried out to God to be delivered; after freeing them; they forgot about God and began to pervert themselves again. This process continued for several generations, each time the succeeding generation did not effectively communicate the knowledge of God; in the absence of this teaching and testimonials about the faithfulness of God, the next generation did not have anything to sustain them and were easily corrupted. Hence, God was not pleased and this is why He continued to allow them to be taken captive. They never applied faith and wisdom outside of captivity; faith brought them out, but wisdom was going to keep them out. Nonetheless, once you have a plan then you must put faith and wisdom to action.

Faith and Wisdom in Action

This brings us to the second point: faith and wisdom in action. God may have given you a vision and detailed specifications on an idea that would revolutionize the world; this still does not mean you need to go out an immediately do it. I know this sister in the Lord who had been ministered to concerning her future as a missionary. She was told she would be a missionary to a foreign nation and that God would use her to bring healing to the land. Immediately, she

The Roots of Faith and Wisdom

quit her job and effectively packed her bags to get ready; the problem was that the prophecy spoke to her future as a missionary and the time had not yet come for her to go to the missionary field. She still had more developing and training to experience before being equipped for ministry. Unfortunately, since she had quit her job and no longer had a means of income, she quickly fell into financial difficulty. She learned some valuable lessons regarding time, season and patience in this process that will be applicable in the ministry. However, God did not allow her to fall to far and she is on course to prosper in God, but now she is using faith and wisdom. It was not that she did not have faith; her failure was not getting and applying the wisdom from the Lord. Getting wisdom from the Lord is crucial to a successful life in Him.

In 1 Samuel 30:1-8, it is recorded that the Amalekites had raided and burned Ziklag and had taken captive the wives and children of David and his men. Although saddened and bitter in spirit, David found strength in the Lord. In verse 8 David inquired of the Lord, "Shall I pursue this raiding party? Will I overtake them?" He sought the Lord's wisdom. David did not get mad and immediately run after them because they took from him; David sought wisdom from God. Still in verse 8 the Lord says to David, "Pursue them, you will certainly overtake them and succeed in the rescue." We have to get the mind of the Lord before our emotions (or logic) lead us in the wrong direction. The premise is this, not every good idea is from God. Hence, we must join our faith with Godly wisdom. James 1:5 says, "If any of you lacks wisdom, he should ask God, who gives generously to all without finding fault, and it will be given to him." We have faith; a mustard seed or measure of faith (whatever we have is enough), but we were given limitless amounts of wisdom. Sadly, we often use all the faith and ignore the wisdom when taking action. The biblical example of this was committed by Joshua.

In Joshua 9, the Gibeonites used wisdom to save their lives because they heard of what God had done to Jericho

The Roots of Character

and Ai through Joshua and the Israelites. The Gibeonites' wisdom amounted to a lie, but was effective because the Israelites did not use wisdom. The people of Gibeon went to see Joshua with donkeys that had wornout sacks, the men put on worn and patched sandals and wore old clothes; they even packed old, dry and moldy bread and carried old wineskins. Once they were in the Israelites camp, the Gibeonites said that they had come from a very distant country and that their bread was fresh when they started this journey. The men of Israel sampled their provisions, but did not inquire of the Lord. Afterwards, Joshua made a treaty with them that was ratified by the leaders of the assembly. In all this, neither Joshua nor his leaders inquired of the Lord about the Gibeonites and this nonaction by them could have cost them their lives. If God had given a command to destroy everything, then the Israelites would have condemned themselves; amazingly, all they had to do was ask God, "Who are these people?" Since they, more poignantly, Joshua did not ask the Lord about these people, it was considered acceptable to make an oath with them. When three days had passed and they found out these people were their neighbors, i.e., part of the people whose land was to be taken, the people became angry and incensed, but were prevented from harming them because of the oath made by the leaders. The whole assembly grumbled against the leaders and they replied "We can not touch them." Even when you make the mistake of not getting the wisdom of God, you are still bound by the integrity of your word.

Often, in the name of wisdom and like the Gibeonites, children of God tell lies. Telling someone that you are going to be at a certain place at a certain time, when you know that you are not, is a lie. Omitting the key facts in a report is a lie. Santa Claus is a lie! Pretending that you do not want something, when you do is a lie. Speaking things into existence that are not as if they were, is a lie if you do not believe the words. It does not matter if your intentions are good; to mislead someone to spare their feelings is a

The Roots of Faith and Wisdom

lie. This does not mean to blurt out a cold, hard truth as wisdom needs to be applied in all forms of communication. Matthew 5:37 says, "Simply, let your 'Yes' be 'Yes' and your 'No,' 'No'; anything beyond this comes from the evil one." If your words can be accepted, then so can your warnings. As children of God, we should speak to promote the integrity of God's Word and because we believe.

Allow me to clarify something, as I return to faith and wisdom in action. Joshua and the Israelites demonstrated the heart of God and had compassion on the Gibeonites; they examined the condition of their clothes, sandals and bags, thereby concluding that they must be telling the truth. Always remember, that things are not always as they appear. They could not have imagined that someone would go to such great lengths to deceive; ironically, they did not have to draw any conclusions at all, they only needed to ask the Lord. You have to get the mind of the Lord and allow Him to determine your actions. As you build your relationship with God, you will come to know God intimately, but this still should not preclude your inquiry of the Lord. Remember the steps of a righteous man are ordered by God; this means that as long as you are in right standing with God, then your obedience and actions will be tied into the Holy Spirit; you may get the answer you seek without even verbalizing the question; sometimes you merely need to get before the Lord to hear what He is saying. God will be with you no matter what step you take as His desire is not for you to go down a wrong path, but it sure is a whole lot better to know that God is with you and that you are on the right path. As it relates to getting the mind of the Lord, your silence can communicate with God better than your questions.

In John 8, a woman caught in adultery was brought before Jesus and the people gathered in the temple courts. The teachers of the law and the Pharisees asked Jesus, "In the Law, Moses commanded us to stone such women. Now what do you say?" They were attempting to trap Jesus by getting Him to speak against the Law, but Jesus merely stooped to the ground and began to write with His finger; a stall tactic perhaps as He did not immediately respond to them. As they continued to question Him, he stood up and said, "If any one of you is without sin, let him be the first to throw a stone at her." Jesus then returned to writing on the ground. This is the power of silence. By not immediately answering Jesus, not only maintained control of himself, but also had the opportunity to talk to the Father about how to answer them. I am certain that the Pharisees and teachers of the Law were becoming frustrated with Jesus as He remained silent. When Jesus broke His silence, He spoke with power, simplicity, conviction and wisdom from God that silenced His accusers, thereby causing them to disperse; he did not have to address them again, but returned to His silence and allowed His words to echo in the hearts of the people. Once wisdom, God's wisdom, is spoken, there is no need to explain. Obtaining Godly wisdom is essential to taking the proper action and the proper action epitomizes the reality of faith. This notion is best supported by the words recorded in James 2:21-22, 24 "Was not our ancestor Abraham considered righteous for what he did when he offered his son Isaac on the altar? You see that his faith and his actions were working together, and his faith was made complete by what he did. You see that a person is justified by what he does and not by faith alone."

Faith and Wisdom in Speech

The third component is faith and wisdom in speech. Proverbs 22:11 says that "He who loves a pure heart and whose speech is gracious will have the king for his friend." Of course you have to determine how important it is to have the king for a friend; as stated earlier nothing should cause or compromise the integrity of your relationship with God. Nonetheless, as it relates to purity of heart and gracious speech, it is certainly in your best interest to honor those in authority over you. You do not want to

The Roots of Faith and Wisdom

encourage the wrath of the king. To exemplify this point, let us take a look at King David. David was an awesome man of God; he had successfully fought a lion and bear, killing them with his bare hands and is referred to as a man after God's own heart. Although he was not asked or instructed, God was important enough to him that he wanted to build God a temple in which to dwell. David was the author of most of the Psalms, each with its own particular brand of reverence toward God. Despite all this, King David had a habit of killing the people who brought him bad news; this is why you do not want to anger the king.

As a point of reference, the Israelites through the prophet Samuel, petitioned God for a king to rule over them. Samuel told them what would happen if they had a king, but they ignored his warnings; the Lord gave them up to their request and said to give them a king. Saul became king of the Israelites; he ruled fairly well until he disobeyed a command of the Lord. The Lord told Saul to attack the Amalekites and totally destroy everything that belongs to them. Saul spared the army of Agag and kept the best of the sheep, cattle, fat calves and lambs. Samuel told Saul that since he rejected the Lord that the Lord will also reject him and that his kingdom had been torn from his hands. David was anointed to replace Saul as king. The Spirit of the Lord left Saul and an evil spirit came upon him. David, after killing Goliath, found favor with Saul and became his armor bearer. Whatever Saul gave David to do, he did it so successfully that David was promoted; eventually the people praised David more than Saul. This caused Saul to become increasingly jealous of David.

Afterwards, Saul repeatedly tried to kill David; even to the point of searching for him and chasing him throughout the country. David had a couple of opportunities to kill Saul, but would not touch God's anointed despite what Saul was trying to do to him. Saul, even while searching and trying to kill David, was in a losing battle with the Philistines; ultimately he tried to take his own life to avoid capture. Saul managed to only wound himself and was still alive when an Amalekite came upon him and quickly took his life. Also, Ishboreth, Saul's son, was killed by servants of David, as he lay in his bed resting. In both instances, the Amalekite and the two who killed Ishboreth, Recab and Baanah were ordered to be killed by David. David's position is summarized in 2 Samuel 4:9, "As surely as the Lord lives, who has delivered me out of all trouble, when a man told me, 'Saul is dead,' and thought he was bringing good news, I seized him and put him to death in Ziklag. That was the reward I gave him for his news! How much more, when wicked men have killed an innocent man in his own house and on his own bed, should I not now demand his blood from your hand and rid the earth of you!" As you read through this, it is obvious David did not kill them for just bringing bad news. They were killed because they did not fear God and were without honor, respectively. Nonetheless, what do you think would happen to the person who tells David that his son, Absalom, is dead? The answer would depend on whether the messenger would use faith and wisdom in speech.

Now Absalom, like Saul, had also turned on David using his own brand of wisdom to gain the favor and hearts of the Israelites; his actions were all part of a master plan to overthrow King David. Absalom had obtained enough devotion to where he could stage a coo; when King David heard of this he decided to flee from Absalom for he was going to kill King David. Despite Absalom's intentions, David the father did not want his son harmed. He said to his men in 2 Samuel 18:5, "Be gentle with the young man Absalom for my sake." Unfortunately for Absalom, one of David's men, Joab, was not going to honor his wishes. Absalom was riding a mule and when the mule had gone underneath the thick branches of a large oak, Absalom's head was caught in the tree. He was left hanging in midair while the mule kept going. Joab had come upon Absalom and plunged three javelins into his heart while Absalom was still alive in the tree; then ten of Joab's armor bearers joined in on the

The Roots of Faith and Wisdom

kill. After all this someone had to tell David that his son was dead.

There was a young man named Ahimaaz whose job was to intermittently report messages back to the king. However, on this occasion as recorded in 2 Samuel 18:20, Joab told Ahimaaz that "You are not the one to take the news today." Then Joab said to a Cushite, "Go tell the king what you have seen." Joab was protecting Ahimaaz because he knew that King David would kill the messenger of bad news; also, Joab had to know that the Cushite had wisdom and therefore believed him to be the better man to deliver the message to King David. However, Ahimaaz was relentless in his pursuit and was determined to run; again Joab inquired of him, "Why do you want to run?" There is no good news to report. Ahimaaz's response in verse 23 of 2 Samuel 18, was "Come what may, I want to run." Ahimaaz was more impressed with his ability to run than the message that he would carry. Joab, apparently worn out by the pestering of Ahimaaz granted him permission to run and although he was to run behind the Cushite, Ahimaaz took a short cut and outran the Cushite. As Ahimaaz approached the city, the watchman called out to the king and reported it. The king said that if he is running alone, then he must have good news; King David also said the same thing about the Cushite who was also seen running. Keep in mind that David, the father, did not want his son killed and was already grieved over Absalom's rebellion and perhaps knew that his death was a possibility. Hence, this was an extremely sensitive time for David and he really needed to hear some good news concerning his son.

2 Samuel 18:28-29 records these words, "Then Ahimaaz called out to the king, 'All is well!' He bowed down before the king with his face to the ground and said, "Praise be to the Lord your God! He has delivered up the men who lifted their hands against my lord the king." The king asked, "Is the young man Absalom safe?" Ahimaaz, in a nutshell said to the king, "I don't know." The most important thing to David was the safety of his son. Despite his experience

and knowledge of the shortcut, he did not have the right information. Ahimaaz ran by faith, but did not have the wisdom of speech to be trusted to deliver the message; if Ahimaaz had known that Absalom was dead, he most likely would have just said, "No, he is dead!" This response would have resulted in his death. In verse 30, the king tells Ahimaaz to step aside as he waited for the Cushite to arrive. Hear the wisdom as stated by the Cushite in verses 31 and 32, "My lord the king, hear the good news! The Lord has delivered you today from all who rose up against you." The king asked the Cushite, "Is the young man Absalom safe?" The Cushite replied, "May the enemies of my lord the king and all who rise up to harm you be like that young man." He honored the king in telling him the good news about his enemies; additionally he honor and respected regarding the death of Absalom; the Cushite even saved his own life through his sensitivity. The Cushite had a pure heart and wisdom in speech; he was not the most experienced when it came to running, but he sure knew how to deliver a message. It is not enough to run with a message you have to know how to deliver it. The giving of this message allowed David to receive the news of his son's death without killing the messenger.

Faith and Wisdom in Giving

Beyond the giving of messages, faith and wisdom in giving brings about the glory of God. This giving specifically relates to the releasing of your money for the work of the Kingdom. It is quite admirable for someone to completely trust God with their finances and be obedient in sacrificial giving. However, there is a difference, a big difference, between writing a check in faith and writing a faith check. A check in faith says that the money has been earmarked for some other purpose, but you decide to trust God to meet your needs. Hence, you may take your savings or retirement money and give it to the Lord. The key component is that you actually have the money. A faith

The Roots of Faith and Wisdom

check is where you do not have the money, but write a check anyway. Now, there is nothing wrong with trusting God, but God is not going to drop money from heaven to cover your bad check. The angels in heaven did not have a ball to play with, so they gathered up all those bouncing checks! When it is time to give to the Lord, God looks at the heart. If you decide to write a check to God and you know you do not have the money and the check is returned, you have just broken a vow to God; your signature is a good faith representation that this check is worth something. With a check, you are saying Lord I am giving take this check for the work of the kingdom; take it Lord and use it. The Lord accepts your gift and has a representative take it to the bank; the bank returns the check because the check is worth nothing as there are not enough funds in the bank to cover it. The work of the Kingdom may be negatively impacted because you wanted to stand in the giving line. We have to exercise wisdom in our giving, but more importantly we have to realize that on a given day, at a specific point in time, you may not have money. God loves a cheerful giver, not one who feels guilty about not giving. It is better to count up all the change in the coin holder in your car and present that to the Lord, than it is to write a thousand dollar check that will not clear the bank; in fact, it would be better to present yourself to the Lord instead of writing a bad check. In the latter case, you have not given anything and rather than exercise your faith, you are promoting your excitement.

Giving out of excitement yields nothing, but being excited about giving has great rewards. This kind of excited giving usually takes place at conferences, especially prophetic conferences. Jumping up to get in line to receive the blessings from God with a check that has the elasticity of a super ball; you know you do not have the money so why stand up in front of God saying that you do. The anointing of this powerful minister of the gospel can be negated by rubber checks. Besides prophecies are conditional upon your consistent walk and development in God and since

The Roots of Character

you just manipulated the prophet through false promises, you have negatively impacted promises of God. The main thing that needs to be exercised is your wisdom. There will always be needs so the one that is presented before you should not cause you to stumble in faith by trying to give what you do not have. To make this clearer, you can not give a check on Sunday and then call the church to have them hold the check on Monday. There are those who do this and then get upset when they find out that the moneys were night deposited. What do you mean you went to the bank already? The money should be able to be taken to the bank, after all when you gave it you said it was good. Do not misinterpret this discussion; you should give out of your need in order to prove God or for God to prove himself, but you have to have it before you can give it. Ecclesiastes 11:1 reads, "Cast your bread upon the waters for after many days you will find it" and verse 6a says, "Sow your seed in the morning . . ." In both instances the bread and the seed, respectively, are in the possession of the giver awaiting release. Luke 6:38, echoes this point; it says "Give, and it will be given to you." Something can only be released or given once it is in your possession or you have established ownership.

Now, there are times when you may be asked to give and it does not make since to your rationale mind to do so; this asking is at the prompting of the Holy Spirit. I remember when my church was in a building drive and families were challenged in faith to give three thousand dollars by the end of the year. During the month of April, my wife and I were in the process of buying our first home. Nonetheless, we accepted this challenge and since we were saving money for the down payment the first thousand was easy, especially considering we still were several months away from the closing on the house. The next thousand was a little more difficult, but we were holding fast to our faith. Remember in the acknowledgments when I said my wife seems to already know God is saying; when I mentioned to my wife about that third thousand, we were

The Roots of Faith and Wisdom

roughly two months from closing, she looked at me and I knew God was asking me had I lost my mind. The wisdom of her silence told me that I better leave this subject alone. Legitimately, what I was suggesting did not make sense to her and she did not have a problem with letting me know that it did not make sense. However, I knew that the devil does not and would not say give to the church. If you have ever had a prompting in your spirit or have been in a position to release to someone what God has given you, rest assured this is not the devil. In fact, you can determine if it is really God prompting your giving by asking this question: Does this make sense? If the answer is no, then it is probably God. This experience is a tangible form of *His ways are not are ways!* Nonetheless, I thank God for his faithfulness because He made a way such that I could earn the thousand dollars outside of our regular household income and fulfill the commitment we made to the church. We praise Him all the more because, we even had extra money to use for our home.

There is one particular form of giving that causes difficulty for many; in real terms, it is not giving at all, it is the paying tithes. Paying tithes is the release into God's house one tenth of your increase. This is the gross increase and not the take home amount. Personally, my wife and I did not always tithe, but once we started tithing, I absolutely refused to stop and this could have potentially left us sitting in the dark. We would not have literally been in the dark, but we would have been late on an electric bill. My wife and I made a commitment to be and live debt free; we progressed nicely through the elimination of the credit cards that were in our names. We had done such a good job we had positioned ourselves to buy the house ahead of schedule, but before we were completely debt free. After moving into the house, we refocused our efforts on becoming debt free. As we zealously pursued our goal, we found ourselves in the position of deciding between paying our tithes and offerings and paying our light bill. Fortunately, my wife figured out an agreeable method to do both, because not paying God our tithes was not an option. She is a wise woman.

Ecclesiastes 7:11-12 reads, "Wisdom, like an inheritance, is a good thing and benefits those who see the sun. Wisdom is a shelter, as money is a shelter, but the advantage of knowledge is this; that wisdom preserves the life of its possessor." Furthermore, Proverbs 4:5-7 says, "Get wisdom, get understanding; do not forget my words or swerve from them. Do not forsake wisdom, and she will protect you; love her, and she will watch over you. Wisdom is supreme; therefore get wisdom. Though it cost you all you have, get understanding." See, faith and wisdom really are intertwined and whereas we should fight the good fight of faith, we should use the weapon of wisdom. As children of God, not only do you have to recognize the importance of faith, but also that the fear of the Lord is the beginning of wisdom; a wisdom that is essential to our life in Christ. Finally, James 3:13 reads, "Who is wise and understanding among you? Let him show it by his good life, by deeds done in the humility that comes from wisdom."

The Roots of Discipline

The greatest description of discipline that I have ever seen or heard is found in Hebrews 12:11; it reads, "No discipline seems pleasant at the time, but painful. Later on, however, it produces a harvest of righteousness and peace for those who have been trained by it." To paraphrase, discipline may be tough, but it produces for those who implement it. It is through discipline that visions are accomplished and through the absence of discipline that fantasies or dreams take permanent residence. This discipline is not the correcting or chastising discipline, but one that is a byproduct of determination and forerunner to achieving goals. Also, this type of discipline overrides all feelings.

You may not feel like cutting the grass or washing the car or cleaning the bathroom; you may not feel like going to work or church or even praying. Discipline, like serving God, has nothing to do with how you feel. Abraham could not have felt like sacrificing his son Isaac. Jesus, in the Garden of Gethsemane, did not feel like going to the cross as indicated by Him asking God to take this cup from him or translated, I do not want to do this, so please would you take the burden off my shoulders. Furthermore, Moses did not feel like leaving his family after his father died. In these instances, each man ignored how they were feeling to obey God; they were disciplined and each did what they knew they had to do to please God. If we did things in accordance to how we felt, we would most likely be a miserable people. To avoid becoming miserable, discipline must be added to your foundation; thereby you establish a platform for change.

Change is a necessary and scary phenomenon and is as much a part of development as studying a lesson. For

The Roots of Character

example, the one thing that regularly happens on a job after you have established a firm proficiency for your current responsibilities, is that you get promoted (at least that is what it is called) to another position. A position, most often, where you have no comfort whatsoever; the only thing you have going for you is past success in a job that seemingly has nothing to do with your new responsibilities. Notice the word *seemingly* in the previous sentence; discipline is an element that transcends position and responsibility. It has more to do with the mental state of the person versus the position that you hold. The discipline used to train in the armed forces, is the same discipline that allows for civilian success; the discipline used to run a race is the same discipline that allows you to study for a test; the discipline used to achieve in the workplace is the same discipline that brings success in the home (or vice versa). In each instance, the change is in the ability to refocus and not in the idea that you are doing something unrelated or different. In ministry, the discipline found in tending sheep is the same faithful discipline that affords you, say, the pastorate. The premise is that it is not what you do, but how you do it and what you learn from it. The lessons learned from meaningless activities could be the very thing that propels you to greatness in God.

David's mastery of the slingshot allowed him to defeat Goliath. He had the confidence and faith in God to fight, but he did not have the skill to use the conventional weapons of war and therefore relied on what he knew. David did not go outside of his experiences, even at King Saul's urging, to fight Goliath. By staying with what he knew, David could focus all his attention on defeating Goliath. He did not have to be concerned with anything because he stayed within himself, meaning that he relied on what he knew as oppose to what was popular or normal for battle. Discipline will often put you in a position to stand alone, at a minimum to exercise determination and focus that raises your maturity level and decision making; with this in mind, the

The Roots of Discipline

following discussion is of three components of discipline: preparation, patience, and productivity.

Preparation

A key component to preparation is independence; this is the independence of maturity and determination. For example, years ago in the summer following my freshman year in undergraduate school, I began to fully embrace my independence. For so long, I felt as though what I wanted to do was always subject to someone else; again this is not about becoming obstinate, but more so of becoming self reliant. Self reliance or independence is crucial to discipline. If you felt as though you had to belong to some group or association or even to be part of the in crowd, then you could possibly be setting yourself up to fall victim to peer pressure, drug pressure, foolishness pressure or any other kind of pressure. However, as you establish independence and begin to accept responsibility for your actions, you begin to chart your course of discipline that will allow you to do whatever you want to do in life. It takes two independent persons to become interdependent or mutually dependent. In marriage, this is where two can coexist; willingly giving themselves to the other. If one is dependent on another to affirm their existence, then this person is susceptible to control and manipulation. Hence, the feeling that I had of being subject to someone else was based on a great need for acceptance, even if the acceptance meant I was going to do some things that I would not normally do or even wanted to do.

Again, as I was beginning to establish my independence, I wanted to go to the movies and did not have a way to get there. I asked one of the neighborhood guys to give me a ride to the theater and he said that he did not feel like riding out there; the theater was only about six miles from where we lived. I asked a few times, even offered to pay for gas, all to no avail. I was disappointed because this was something I wanted to do and was effectively being told that I can not do it. This night I would establish within myself that I was not going to be subject to the whims of another. I jogged to the theater, but more importantly I ran into independence. In hindsight, a visionary was born that night because I would no longer allow anyone to tell me what I could not do; I was really becoming like my mother now. However, you need to discipline your independence in every area of your life: physical, social, mental and moral.

Physically, you must learn to take control over your body. This is a lifelong process as suggested by Paul in 1 Corinthians 9:27 where he says, "I beat my body and make it my slave so that after I have preached to others, I myself will not be disqualified for the prize." Do not consider yourself exempt if you are not a preacher, for this is not limited to a pulpit preaching, but more so how your life testifies about what you are doing, the promises you have made to yourself or even who God is to you. For example, if you want to lose weight or just get in better shape, then you need only remember that not everything comes by prayer and fasting; this kind comes by sweat and exercise. In context, 1 Corinthians 6:19 relates to sexual sins when it asks "Do you not know your body is a temple of the Holy Spirit?" However, it also relates to physical weight. Simply put, it is more difficult for people who are obese to be as active for God as they can be; this is not to say that obese people can not be effective for God, but as committed as they may be, physically they may not be able to handle all the demands of ministry that may come their way. Furthermore, when obese people go to the doctor, one of the first things the doctor says is, "You need to lose some weight or you will be putting yourself at risk." Afterwards, they inquire about eating habits, diet, and frequency of exercise; in other words, doctors want to know if you are applying any discipline to your life. Being large does not mean that you have more of the Holy Spirit; it does mean that you may not have the energy to allow the Holy Spirit to fully use you.

The Roots of Discipline

Allow me to interject a side note: small, perpetual errors in judgment result in a lack of discipline. For example, two people, over the course of a year eat the same thing every day; one is eating a salad and the other is eating a hamburger (assume this is their total diet). Initially there is no difference, but as the year progresses, as time moves on there will be a tangible difference. These little decisions are made every day without regard to the big impact they are having; most of the time, it is just a little bit of this or a small bite or a couple of chips; in other words, if you have enough pennies, you can become a millionaire. I am not trying to upset anyone with this discussion and am aware that big or large people are not necessarily unhealthy. They can, at times, even do more than thin people, but this is not about comparing. This is about how well you take care of your physical body, big, small, fat or thin. No matter what category you are in it is possible to be unhealthy and out of shape. Since you body houses the Holy Spirit, this writing is to encourage you to add discipline to your physical habits.

Nonetheless, protecting your body is not limited to the physical and therefore you must watch who you interact with to protect your mind or guard against negative influences. Socially, you must be selective in your interactions. 1 Corinthians 15:33 says "Bad company corrupts good character." To paraphrase, the depth of your character is measured by the company you keep. When high school graduates go off to college and return to the neighborhood, often they do not look at the neighborhood the same. The neighborhood use to be the whole world and now they realize that there is more. The exposure to new surroundings opened up the world to these bright minds; this is not to say that the old neighborhood is full of bad people, it is to say that the new surroundings have allowed for new possibilities. Please understand you can, even in college, still end up being affected by negativity (and in many cases the opportunity is greater), but you also have a larger segment from which to observe and choose.

The decision making process will never become more evident or necessary than when facing a new environment, be it college, moving to a new city or perhaps getting a new job. The more you are exposed, the more choices that will lie before you, especially in choosing a mate or getting married. The bible says in 2 Corinthians 14, "Do not be yoked together with unbelievers. For what do righteousness and wickedness have in common? Or what fellowship can light have with the darkness." Spiritually, this means that two should believe the same, both being followers of Christ. However, just because two people are Christians, does not mean they are equally yoked. 2 Thessalonians 3:6 says, "In the name of the Lord Jesus Christ, we command you, brothers, to keep away from every brother who is idle and does not live according to the teaching . . ." To interpret, if a brother (or sister) is not doing right by God, then you are under no obligation, spiritual or otherwise, to fellowship with them and should keep your distance lest whomever causes you to become idle. Thus, as the saying goes, an idle mind is the devil's playground.

This leads to the third area of your life to apply discipline: mentally. An advertisement says that a mind is a terrible thing to waste; there is great truth to this and it had a biblical basis. 2 Corinthians 5:17 says, "If anyone is in Christ, he is a new creation; the old has gone, the new has come." This scripture is referring to the renewing of the mind but this renewal, based on faith, must be protected by discipline. Romans 12:2-3 says, "Do not conform any longer to the pattern of the world, but be transformed by the renewing of your mind. Then you will be able to test and approve what God's will is, His good, pleasing and perfect will." Transformation does not come easily, but it is something that you must seek after; this is, in part, what is meant in the book of Matthew when it says to "Seek first the Kingdom of God and His righteousness, and all these things shall be added to you." These things refer to that which would cause stress or pressure in trying to obtain; the bible says not to be concerned with what you

The Roots of Discipline

will eat, drink or wear for God has made every provision for you. Since you do not have to be concerned with the necessities, then you can focus on God. Thereby, your mind is renewed and protected.

In addition to being strong and courageous and the promise that He will be with him wherever he goes, God tells Joshua in Joshua 1:8, to meditate on His word day and night. Meditation is part of the renewal process; the things that are in your mind that are not of God will be pushed out by the Word of God as you mentally digest the revelation of God. Remember, light and dark can not occupy the same spot. In 2 Timothy 2:15, the bible says to "Do your best to present yourself to God as one approved, a workman who does not need to be ashamed and who correctly handles the Word of truth." Again, as you study the Word or other books whose foundation is the Word (for deeper clarity) then your mind will be renewed and you become more stable concerning the things of God.

This notion of stability leads to the final area of discussion of discipline: morality. Specifically, moral discipline as it relates to sex, money, and power. Before I proceed, one of the things a disciple of Christ must learn to do is mind their own business. Unfortunately, there is a tendency to look outward at someone else's problem as opposed to looking at the potential mess in your own life. A rose of any color is still a rose; likewise gossip, even if disguised as gathering specific information for prayer is still gossip. I used to think that women were the big gossips but not any more; I have seen plenty of men who can hold their own on the gossip mill. Nonetheless, since God reveals to redeem, the next time God reveals something to you about someone, your responsibility is to pray that situation through. God showed it to you because He trusted you to intercede on behalf of the person. The only time you should open your mouth about something that has been revealed to you is when you are about to pray; otherwise, as stated in 1 Thessalonians 4:12, "Make it your ambition to lead a

The Roots of Character

quiet life, to mind your own business and to work with your hands, just as you were told . . ."

Notwithstanding, sexual sins are perhaps the most pervasive in the world; lust is the process of desiring something that you do not need or should not have and is a prerequisite to sexual sins. This is why people do not just happen to commit adultery or fornicate; at some point, the thought crossed their minds and depending on what they did with that thought determines whether or not a sexual sin is committed. A noteworthy item is that you do not have to physically have sex to commit adultery; the bible says that if a man even looks at a woman, he has committed adultery in his heart. Obviously, he would be doing more than looking in his mind. Another thing to note is that God always has a way out should you find yourself in a predicament, but it will take even greater discipline to walk away from that which you have already mentally experienced. However, as stated in 1 Thessalonians 4:3-6, "It is God's will that you should be sanctified: that you should avoid sexual immorality; that each of you should learn to control his own body (here is that physical part again) in a way that is holy and honorable, not in passionate lust like the heathen, who do not know God; and that in this matter no one should wrong his brother or take advantage of him . . ." Not only is this God's will, but it should also become our will; let this be your mandate and receive this affirmation: I respect and honor all established covenants, including God's covenants and the covenants between husband and wife.

The second point on moral discipline concerns money. You may recall the discussion of the purpose of money in chapter *The Root of Giving*, but as it relates to discipline I offer this warning: be careful how you love, it may lead you to destruction. 1 Timothy 6:7-10 says, "For we brought nothing into the world, and we can take nothing out of it. But if we have food and clothing, we will be content with that. People who want to get rich fall into temptation and a trap and into many foolish and harmful desires that plunge

The Roots of Discipline

men into ruin and destruction. For the love of money is a root of all kinds of evil. Some people, eager for money, have wandered from the faith and pierced themselves with many griefs."

The final point on moral discipline is power. God has given us power over serpents and scorpions; the power over the enemy and the power to make mountains move; no matter how it is used, we have the power of faith. However, as a function of moral discipline, this is not the power in question; the power in question relates to dominion. The Book of Genesis records that man was given power to rule and have dominion, but that was over animals and not people. Although man was given rule over woman, he was not given the power to dominate woman.

In Ephesians 5:23-24 the bible says, "For the husband is the head of the wife as Christ is the Head of the church, of which He is the Savior. Now wives should submit to their husbands in everything." If I am to interpret this correctly, then as Christ is to the church, a provider, safe haven, assurance, peace, comfort, resting place, so is the husband to the wife. As head of the household, the husband has the responsibility to maintain a pleasant and peaceful home.

Naturally speaking, if a wife is not fulfilled in the home, then the husband is not doing what he is supposed to do as the head. Being the head does not mean you have the power to put you foot down; it means that you have the responsibility to reach down and pick up anyone in the home who may be down (whether by prayer or otherwise). Being the head does not mean that every decision is yours to make; it means that you need the wisdom to know when you are not wisest person on a given subject and trust your wife's decision. Finally, being the head does not mean that when you are tired from a long day's work that you get to rest. It means that you must be supportive, considerate and understanding to the needs of your wife. For the single persons reading this, you have the responsibility to do these things for yourself until, if you desire, you have a spouse in which to share your understanding of moral discipline. However, just like everything else, this type of discipline takes time.

Patience

Inherent to this time component is the discipline of patience. Imagine the formation of the stone that David used to kill Goliath. Through the long acts of nature, this compressed sand and water shaped stone would have a place history. The pressure applied from the loosening ground and the ripples in a flowing stream would position this stone for greatness. Now, imagine the impatience connected to this development. If the stone could speak, it may wish that it would grow faster, but would complain of all the pressure. It may become weary of the running water that was changing its shape and wish that it would stop. It may feel as though it did not deserve any of these storms because they only caused the ground to shift and more water to flow. The stone may not have had much patience with its development, but in the process of time the stone was able to fulfill its purpose and help David kill Goliath. Unfortunately, many of us do not realize that the pressures and storms of life are designed to promote our development. We merely need to look beyond the current condition and learn from those storms, but this requires patience.

Patience itself almost becomes a phenomenon. Recently a friend of mine was describing to me how she was not going to pray for patience because everything starts to go wrong when you pray that prayer. As I thought about what she was saying, I concluded that she did not want to be all she can be in God because it was going to be a little difficult. Nonetheless, the reality is that every day, with or without prayer, we are faced with situations that test our patience. As for me, I did not have much patience for anything and in the process of time I was able to learn patience. Notwithstanding, when I grew tired, I had no

The Roots of Discipline

patience whatsoever and responded accordingly. Basically, to be tired is to be completely out of patience; early in the day, loud music or a long stop light or constant interruptions may not be a problem, but these same occurrences late in the evening are nerve racking. The difference is that you are now tired. When I became tired, I did not reflect the love of God as described earlier; in case you are wondering, yes my wife did help me see this.

    I did not like the person I became when I was tired; a disciple is a disciple no matter the conditions. I had to master tiredness and so I created my own set of tests to improve in this area. Intermittently, over a period of about six months, I would stay up late and get up early this was so I would be tired going through the day. The purpose was to handle myself appropriately even when tired. This exercise started off with great failure, but that only served to prove the need. Eventually I began to handle tiredness in the same manner as if I were sufficiently rested. Little did I know that being tired and having the ability to function normally would become so relevant in my life; my son, almost on a daily basis, meets me at the door ready to play. It does not matter that I worked extra hours and was up late the night before; he wants to play with Daddy. As we play and my tiredness increases, I can not lose patience, although I may look at the clock and wonder if it is bedtime. By definition, patience is the ability to deal with problems without complaining or becoming angry. Discipline says this is what I have to do and I am going to do it and patience adds, do it as if you were well rested, even if you are not. Please do not misunderstand, when you are tired you should call on God more to help get you through your storm. Psalms 50:15 says, "Call upon me in the day of trouble and I will surely answer you." There is no greater trouble than to be tired and have a wealth of things to do involving other people. Also, when you are tired your discipline has to tell you when you have had enough; there are times when you just have to get some rest.

Another situation where patience is heavily tested in is waiting; somehow when it comes to waiting every second becomes an eternity. For example, you ring a doorbell and before the sound can finish resonating, you are ready to go or looking through the window to see if someone is coming. It may feel like it is taking two hours, but in actuality it has not even been a minute. Unfortunately, the more tired you are, the longer the wait appears to be. The Lord reminds us through the prophet Isaiah that those who wait upon the Lord will renew their strength; eventually they will soar with eagles. Ironically, this suggests that you can save more time by waiting. Taking the time to utilize what God had given you rather than frantically responding to an emergency is discipline. The notion is affirmed in 2 Timothy 4:5, "Keep your head in all situations, endure hardship, do the work of an evangelist, discharge all the duties of your ministry." Everyone has the ministry of reconciliation. As it relates to responding in an emergency, if you lose your head and begin to sympathize with someone, you will be of no good. Your focus and objectivity may become lost in the excitement. Empathy is developing an intuitive understanding about someone's problem. In waiting, the definition given above also incorporates pain; meaning that when you are waiting on the Lord to heal you, there should be no complaining and certainly you should not become angry with God. This is where patience becomes perseverance, the refusal to give up and to hold on to your beliefs.

God will not leave you nor forsake you and He will answer you when you call on Him, but this does not mean God will do it when and how you expect Him. There is added emphasis when you have not learned the lesson from the storm. For example, God would not immediately deliver you from financial problems, if you have not been faithful over the little that you have; this kind does not go by prayer and fasting, but faith and wisdom. Notwithstanding, suppose you have been extremely faithful and diligent in serving God; this does not preempt you from the storms of life. Paul writes in 2 Corinthians 12:7-10, "To keep me

The Roots of Discipline

from becoming conceited because of these surpassingly great revelations, there was given me a thorn in my flesh, a messenger of Satan, to torment me. Three times I pleaded with the Lord to take it away from me. But He said to me 'My grace is sufficient for you, for my power is made perfect in weakness.' Therefore, I will boast all the more gladly about my weaknesses, so that Christ's power may rest on me. That is why, for Christ's sake, I delight in weaknesses, in insults, in hardships, in persecutions, in difficulties. For when I am weak, then I am strong." This is a powerful example of persevering. Paul, the great servant of God, had a thorn in his flesh to keep him humble; he only had to wait for God's grace to manifest during those weak times. Concerning the definition of a thorn, the following is an excerpt from another poem I wrote:

> A thorn is that element of humanity
> > That says that you need
> A thorn is an option
> > Not an obligation
> A thorn is a reminder
> > Not a license
> A thorn is an encouragement
> > Not a curse
> A thorn is choice
> > An exercise of power
> A thorn is an opportunity
> > To realized unearned favor

Waiting on God to strengthen you to deal with the pain of a thorn requires patience and perseverance. Another thing that requires this type of discipline is frustration.

To have patience and to persevere when you are mistreated is especially difficult when this mistreatment or frustration comes from your leader. A friend of mine was out ministering with his pastor and something happened; his pastor, perhaps through excitement, literally yelled at him in front of a close friend of his (as if privately it would have been better). He had become so angry and frustrated with this incident. In hindsight, as we talked about it, I would have told him what Ecclesiastes 10:4 says, "If a ruler's anger rises against you, do not leave your post; calmness can lay great error to rest." However, I did tell him that a wise man overlooks insults and that his intended response was not wise; if he had acted when he said, not only would he have lost his head in this situation, but would have made matters worst by responding from an emotional base. It was not his fault that his pastor had not realized or was not treating those who served under him in the ministry like they were also children of God. I have never seen a vision that was able to be accomplished by one person and therefore the people who work with you in the vision need to be respected and appreciated; if correction is warranted, never lose sight that you are correcting a child of God, not to mention a human being with feelings.

Productivity

The final component of discipline is productivity. This is because you can change and still not become effective. Most often this type of change is because someone else changes. For example, imagine a child has two toys in which to play; he spends his time playing with one of the toys and completely ignores the other. Soon thereafter a second child shows up and begins to play with the other toy and now the first child wants the other toy more than the one he had. In this regard, there is no discipline in the first child as indicated by the overwhelming urge to have what the other kid has. For children, this is normal to their development and could be used as an opportunity to teach about sharing. However, with adults or those who have reached the age of responsibility (and it does differ) this change is problematic. To exemplify, suppose God has given you a vision for a computer business. You were given all the plans and specifically instructed not to advertise and that

The Roots of Discipline

God would be your personal marketing director. You obey all the instructions given by God until a competitor opens up a computer business nearby and begins to show signs of success. Naturally, this is attributed to his marketing campaigns and television advertisements. Immediately, you feel as though you have to take out advertisements in order to compete and therefore go against the instructions from God. Changing from obedience to disobedience because of what you see is the beginning of a downward spiral. It is perfectly acceptable to learn from others, but not at the expense of disobeying God. Effectively, you changed your vision or goal to someone else's and therefore became disobedient to what God told you. Disobedience will move you from productive to nonproductive and is the offspring of a lack of discipline. Although the accomplishments of goals are tangible measures of productivity, productivity is not limited to stated goals.

It is possible to demonstrate discipline and be productive without expressly stated goals. However, this type of productivity is the result of a higher goal that demands certain actions. For example, in Matthew 25:35-36, Jesus says, "For when I was hungry you gave me something to eat, I was thirsty and you gave me something to drink, I was a stranger and you invited me in, I needed clothes and you clothed me, I was sick and you looked after me, I was in prison and you came to visit me." Jesus was questioned as to when He was in any of those positions. In verse 40, He responded, "I tell you the truth, whatever you did for one of the least of these brothers of mine, you did for me." Hence, you may not have the stated goal of feeding the hungry, but if you have the goal of becoming Christ like, then you will feed the hungry and clothe the naked and visit those in prison, etc. Jesus did not come for those who have; He came for those who do not. This principle of productivity transcends tangible goals as it embodies a lifestyle of development of Christian character. After all, this is a part of our reasonable service.

The Roots of Character

The discipline of giving to those who can not afford to give back is where the Word of God begins to manifest itself. God works through man and is continually in search of those who will stand in the gap for His people. God will speak to one of His servants to bless another of His servants as an answer to prayer; unless there is a willingness and subsequent obedience to release what you think you need, then someone else's answer to prayer may be delayed. When the bible speaks of Moses having to tell the people to stop giving, he is saying that I recognize your commitment and your discipline, but we have enough for what we need to do for God. It takes discipline and great understanding of who God is to be able to release what you have; you should come to learn that God truly is a God of abundance and He does restore all.

The Roots of Impartation

In Romans 1:11 Paul, in his letter to the Romans, writes "I long to see you so that I may impart to you some spiritual gift to make you strong that is, that you and I may be mutually encouraged by each other's faith." Impartation means to share. 1 Thessalonians 2:8 states, "We loved you so much that we were delighted to share with you not only the gospel of God, but our lives as well, because you had become so dear to us." Impartation also means to disclose or to make known. The closer you get to God, the more He will share with you the revelation of who He is. Luke 3:11 records, "The man who has two tunics should share with him who has none, and the one who has food should do the same." Finally, impartation means to bestow or grant. The bible says that a good man leaves an inheritance for his children's children. The greatest inheritance is spiritual, not monetary. The greatest inheritance is to impart or share your faith and belief in God.

However, it is through the demonstration of belief that someone will receive impartation. Impartation is an affirmation from God and is not based on the laying of hands. The laying of hands, for the purpose of imparting spiritual gifts, was ceremonial. It was an external act that was the manifestation of internal workings or desires. No one has to lay hands on you to receive from God, but you may need this affirming touch or release for the sake of the people that you have been called to serve. In Deuteronomy 34:9 after Moses' death, the bible says, "Joshua son of Nun was filled with the spirit of wisdom because Moses had laid his hands on him." When Moses laid hands on Joshua it was to affirm the culmination of a work that had already taken place. In verse 10, "So the Israelites listened to him and

The Roots of Character

did what the Lord commanded Moses." Moses had passed the torch to Joshua and therefore the people believed in Joshua's leadership.

Joshua's faith in God had been clearly demonstrated. In Numbers 13:26-14:9, the exploration of the land of promise and is discussed. Therein Moses sent twelve spies out to survey what was to become their land. Ten of the twelve did not feel as though they could take this land because of the size of the people in Canaan. However, Joshua and Caleb believed that they could take this land thereby demonstrating complete faith in God. The Israelites talked about stoning Joshua and Caleb. Then, in Numbers 14 verses 23 and 24, the Lord says that ". . . not one of them will ever see the land I promised on oath to their forefathers. No one who has treated me with contempt will ever see it. But because my servant Caleb had a different spirit and follows me wholeheartedly, I will bring him into the land he went to, and his descendants will inherit it." Notice that Joshua, although he demonstrated the same wholehearted faith in God that Caleb did, did not receive an immediate promise of anything. This is because Joshua was expected to believe. Joshua was already Moses' aide and being trained by him; he was already prepared to have faith in God. Caleb received this reward because he caught the revelation of faith from a distance and therefore earned his reward. Effectively, Joshua was supposed to believe because of whom he had already been exposed.

As stated, Joshua was Moses' aide. He went wherever Moses did including the tent of meeting; as described in Exodus 33, the tent of meeting was were the Lord would speak to Moses face to face (heart to heart) as a man speaks to his friend. Afterwards Moses would return to the camp, but Joshua would remain in the tent in the presence of God. It was during these times that Joshua's relationship with God was being established. He began to learn the ways of the Lord and apparently desired more of Him. Joshua also was with Moses on the Mountain of God when Aaron had made the golden calf for idol worship;

The Roots of Impartation

otherwise the Israelites could have accepted Joshua as their leader in Moses' absence and the calf may have never been made. Moses and Joshua were on the mountain of God for forty days. As they were on their way down the mountain, God told Moses of the people's rebellion; Joshua heard the sounds of war, but Moses told him the people were singing. Surprisingly, they were both correct.

Moses stated the truth, while Joshua spoke a revelation. There was a war happening between the flesh and the Spirit (at this point, it appeared as if the Spirit was loosing). Joshua was trained by Moses, but was educated by God. Moses called Joshua, but God affirmed him. In Numbers 27:15, after God told Moses that he would not go to the promise land and that he was about to die, "Moses said to the Lord, 'May the Lord, the God of the spirits of all mankind, appoint a man over this community to go out and come in before them, one who will lead them out and bring them in, so the Lord's people will not be like sheep without a shepherd.'" God said to Moses, in verse 18, "Take Joshua, son of Nun, a man in whom is the Spirit and lay your hand on him." Moses had to have known that Joshua would be the answer to his prayer, but wanted this confirmation from God. Joshua had been in the Lord's presence, had already begun to know His voice and knew how to talk to God; the only thing left to do was to affirm his leadership externally; internally he had already led himself into a deep fellowship with God. The laying of hands was to affirm Joshua's appointment as the leader over the Israelites and to commission him in front of the whole Israelite community; this was so there would be no question as to who the new leader was. Joshua had already demonstrated his love for God and His people; he only needed to continue to develop until he was called upon.

Elisha, like Joshua, was also internally prepared through discipline; however, Elisha's preparation did not come from ministry. God is a God of principles and as long as principles are faithfully followed then God will take notice. Simply stated, you do not have to be serving God to be called by

The Roots of Character

God. For example, Simon (later called Peter) James and John were partners in the fishing business; Jesus happened by one day when they had not caught any fish and told them to cast their nets again. They did so and caught an abundance of fish. Jesus told Simon not to be afraid and that from now on he will catch men. Although Jesus was talking directly to Simon, when they pulled the boats on shore all the business partners followed Jesus. Matthew was also operating a business; he was a tax collector. Tax collectors had to be relentless and disciplined in those days to fulfill their duties; they were not liked for their work (most thieves are not) and were usually in the company of other sinners. Jesus called him while he was sitting at his tax booth. The underlying premise is that it does not matter what you are doing, as long as your heart had not been hardened or was still pliable, God can turn you around and apply the same discipline to the furtherance of His Kingdom. As for Elisha, he too was a business man and was prepared for ministry by running the family business.

Elisha's diligence in business afforded him the opportunity to serve God. Elijah, because he ran from Jezebel, was told by God to anoint Elisha as his successor. 1 Kings 19:19-21, "Elijah went from there and found Elisha son of Shapat. He was plowing with twelve yoke of oxen, and he himself was driving the twelfth pair. This alludes to or implies that there were witnesses to Elisha's calling. Elijah went up to him and threw his cloak around him. Elisha then left his oxen and ran after Elijah. 'Let me kiss my father and mother good-bye' he said, 'and then I will come with you.' 'Go back.' Elijah replied, 'what have I done to you?' So Elisha left him and went back. He took his yoke of oxen and slaughtered them. He burned the plowing equipment to cook the meat and gave it to the people, and they ate. Then he set out to follow Elijah and became his attendant." There are several key points to note within these verses. Elisha was not just a leader by position or family rights; he was also experienced in the literal mechanics of plowing because he was physically involved in

The Roots of Impartation

the process. He was not leading in an area where he had no experience and therefore had the respect of the workers. When Elijah put his cloak around Elisha, immediately there was impartation; the anointing had come over Elisha and he knew that his life had permanently changed. However, before he would follow Elijah he wanted to say goodbye to his parents. Elijah's response was, "What have I done to you?" In other words, *have I done anything to stop you?* This exchange is extremely important because Elisha is doing what he must do by the commandments of God; honor your mother and your father. Now, the bible does not address the conversation that he had with his parents, but implicitly, it had to be laced with humility and respect for his parents. It is necessary, especially when running the family business, to let your parents know that you have not lost your mind, but are responding to the call of God. If Elisha did not go back, he could have brought shame and disgrace on his family; not to mention that confusion and lack of understanding by his parents as to what had happened to their son. The blessings of God are without reproach, even to those to whom you are submitted. Notwithstanding, since Elisha's parents had also become metaphors for that which gives life, then Elisha had to say goodbye to his other parents, the oxen and the plow. By destroying the oxen and plow, he was demonstrating his life's commitment to do the work of the Lord; he removed those things that could have caused him to turn back when things became rough. Elisha had the presence of mind to know that this was not going to be an easy row to hoe.

As Elisha attended to Elijah, like Joshua did to Moses, he most likely experienced some of the greatest tests imaginable; the preparation to become the successor to the prophet who stopped rain for three years and called down fire from heaven must have been incredible. In 2 Kings 2, as the time is nearing for Elijah to be taken up to heaven, Elisha was given the opportunity to not travel on with Elijah; this opportunity was one of Elisha's last few tests for the appointed time was near. Please recall that when Elijah ran from Jezebel, he left his previous attendant and journeyed on through the desert, eventually ending up at the mountain of God; that servant is never mentioned again and I have wondered "What if he had not left Elijah?" For all you armor bearers and attendants, the lesson here is, where your leader goes, you go. Elisha is promised the double portion he asked for if he sees Elijah taken up to heaven. Since Elisha never left Elijah, he was there to pick up the cloak that fell as Elijah was taken up to heaven. Elijah had received the double portion because he had staying power; Elisha was disciplined and again, there was no laying of hands.

Please do not misunderstand, I am aware of the importance of the laying of hands and am not trying to undermine its relevance; however, it is necessary and liberating to remove the limitations surrounding impartation. The laying of hands is vital to our Christian walk as spirits are transferred through the laying of hands; however, since there are good and bad spirits, be careful as to who and what someone may be imparting. Again, the intent is to challenge the thinking that someone has to lay hands on you in order to receive revelation knowledge or power from God. Here is another example, in Luke 8:43-48, a woman who had been bleeding for twelve years came up behind Jesus and touched the edge of his cloak and immediately her bleeding stopped. Jesus knew that someone had touched Him; He also knew it was a different kind of touch. This woman reached out and imparted something to herself. Jesus knew that this power had gone out from Him. After she had come forward, Jesus said to her that her faith had healed her. This woman was healed because she accepted the revelation of God and the attitude of her heart was right. Jesus affirmed the woman's healing, not by touching her, but by speaking the Word. A prepared heart can receive anything from God. Impartation is not tied to anything, but seeking God with your whole heart and thereby developing in relationship with Him; implicit to this is faith and the core belief that God is I am that

The Roots of Impartation

I am. This means that whomever you need God to be at different points in your life that is who he is; when you need a comforter, He comforts; when you need a doctor, He heals; when you need discipline, He corrects. Whatever you have need of that is who God becomes.

Nonetheless, the reference to seeking God is not limited to personal prayer and meditation; a tremendous element to this seeking comes by hearing. Remember, faith comes by hearing and hearing by the Word of God. Every time a preacher stands to minister the Word of God, there is impartation or a sharing of the experiences and revelation of God; the greatest thing that can be imparted is a relationship with God. My former pastor (and hopefully all pastors) imparts with proven precision the revelation of God. When he ministers, you can feel the energy of his belief; a belief that is based on a lifetime of experiencing God. There is such great conviction about God, that he is as exacting as he is long winded (his excitement about God would get the best of him sometimes). His teaching was geared toward focusing the individual on developing their own relationship with God. In contrast, the Israelites told Moses to go and talk to God on their behalf, then come back and tell what He said. They refused to accept responsibility or ownership in seeking after God. Relying on a representative to go before the Lord on your behalf should not be a long term solution (this may exist initially because you may not know how to apply your faith or are just learning) and is inconsistent with what God wants from us. God's original intent was to have fellowship with man; this is indicated by His interaction with Adam prior to the fall (on a side note, Eve fell, Adam laid down). My former pastor is a great servant of God, not because he has seen miracles, but because his ministry is predicated on Jesus' words as found in Matthew 28:19-20a, "Therefore go and make disciples of all nations, baptizing them in the name of the Father and of the Son and of the Holy Spirit, and teaching them to obey everything I have commanded

The Roots of Character

you." However, there were two major things that were imparted to me as my roots were starting to form and that I now share.

The first is that God can use anyone who makes themselves available to Him. On January 18, 1996, I had the occasion to visit with a man of God in his place of seclusion. We began to talk and I shared my doubt about whether or not God would want someone like me. This was based on my developing revelation of who God is and increasing reverence for Him. At this point in my walk with God, I was learning to let go of my past, but had not completed the process and was experiencing negative remorse over the things I had done. Remorse is good as long as you do not allow it to be used against you and this is what was happening to me. The more you learn about God you begin to realize that it does not matter how *big or small* the sin is, just that it all grieves the Holy Spirit; this meant that for the predominant years of my life, I had been grieving Him. This presented great turmoil for me and while tears were streaming down my face, I shared it and received in return a revelation and impartation from God. As recorded in Zechariah 3:1-6 the word of the Lord reads, "Then he showed me Joshua the high priest standing before the Angel of the Lord, and Satan standing at his right side to accuse him. The Lord said to Satan, 'the Lord rebuke you, Satan!' The Lord, who has chosen Jerusalem, rebuke you! Is this not this man a burning stick snatched from the fire?" Now Joshua was dressed in filthy clothes as he stood before the Angel. The Angel said to those who were standing before him, 'take off his filthy clothes.' Then He said to Joshua, 'See, I have taken away your sin, and I will put rich garments on you.' Then I (Zechariah) said, 'Put a clean turban on his head.' So they put a clean turban on his head and clothed him, while the Angel of the Lord stood by. The Angel of the Lord gave this charge to Joshua: This is what the Lord Almighty says: 'If you will walk in my ways and keep my requirements, then you will govern my house and have charge of my courts, and I will give you a place among

The Roots of Impartation

these standing here.' I had already discovered that God is a conditional God and upon receiving this impartation, I knew that I could do anything as long as I remained obedient to God. This bolstered my confidence in the Lord and started me on a path of spiritual freedom. Although I had to deal with my past, per previous chapters, I was not controlled by it. With this impartation, I focused exclusively on God. On subsequent occasions, I would read those verses and substitute my name for Joshua's and become encouraged all over again.

The second impartation is fasting. In Matthew 9:14, Jesus was questioned about fasting, "How is it that we and the Pharisees fast, but your disciples do not fast?" His answer is recorded in verse 15, 'How can the guests of the bridegroom mourn while He is with them?' The time will come when the bridegroom will be taken from them, then they will fast." Although Jesus made these statements, I did not fully grasp the concept until I witnessed the results of a lifestyle of prayer and fasting; I took hold of the principle, personally defined it, and applied it to my life. Fasting is defined as abstaining from food and other physical pleasures for the expressed purpose of developing an intimacy with God; through this intimacy God reveals Himself. If you have the goal to fast to become more powerful or to get more anointing, then you do not understand the principle. This writing discusses two things that fasting does.

Spiritually, fasting allows you to realize or recognize what God has done and is doing in your life. Your strengths and weaknesses are shown to you as you consecrate your body for the Lord. Physically, fasting creates a state of being where you are no longer relying on yourself; your dependency rests completely with God. Understand that this dependency is not like the Israelites who wanted God to continue to send manna from heaven; this dependency is the release of your independence into God's care. As you realize your independence, then you can connect with an independent God. Through this connection, there is

The Roots of Character

interdependence. Simply put, you have come to a place of understanding that God will not violate your will, but wants you to willingly surrender yourself to Him; it is the realization that though you may be resourceful, God is the Source. God depends on man, the independent man, to carry out his purposes here on earth. Man depends on God to be the Source.

Matthew 18:3 records Jesus' words, "I tell you the truth, unless you change and become like little children, you will never enter the Kingdom of heaven." To state the obvious, this does not mean that adults need to regress and become children. Jesus' statements relate to the purity and simplicity of children. Forgiveness is natural for children. Have you ever seen a child become angry and stop speaking to someone? Children do not hold on to wrongful acts and will quickly reinitiate the relationship as they move on. Proverbs 17:9 says, "He who covers an offense promotes love." There is no one better at this than children. Children are also sensitive. I am sure we have observed little children that will warm up nicely to one person and then completely reject someone else; often this is dismissed as shyness, but there are times when there is something wrong and the child knows before the parents. The child may not be able to verbalize what is happening, but will quickly jump in the arms of the person they do know; if the person they want to get away from is still around the child will try to get to mommy or daddy. Becoming like little children means to embrace the attributes of forgiveness and sensitivity (among others). These concepts are highlighted because when fasting, they are intensified.

The more you deny yourself and get closer to God, the more sensitive you become to the things around you. Even the smallest things, like someone's voice, the telephone ringing or perhaps someone standing near you, will bother you greatly. The idea is that you should be able to handle these things with grace, since you are seeking to become more Christ like. Since God shows you who you are when fasting, if you become mean, then this revelation of self is

The Roots of Impartation

something you need to work on. Fasting holds a magnifying glass to your character and therefore is not permission to be mean in the name of sensitivity. If anything, this element of meanness is a component of character that needs to be addressed and not just masked by eating. Imagine climbing God's Holy Mountain and being embraced by Him and then snapping at His people because you are feeling sensitive or tired. This is not the kind of fast the Lord supports. In reality, since you are no longer hiding behind food, you discover just how much grace is operating in your life; now that the crutch is removed and you are no longer able to resist God, you can affirm to God that you have no confidence in the flesh and add personal meaning to Philippians 4:13, "I can do all things through him who gives me strength."

In summary, impartation is like money in that it is only effective if used properly. This means that no matter how charismatic a preacher is or how precise a teacher is, if the ensuing impartation is not applied to your life, then it means nothing. You can have every God serving person on earth lay hands on you or speak into your life, but if you do not stay focused on God and continue to pursue Him, it would all be for nothing. Philippians 4:13 begins, 'I can do . . . ,' this means that your participation is required; it is up to you to take what has been shared and use it to further your development. The gifts given to you by God may not be taken away, but if misused they can go into remission. Proverbs 2:1-5 says, "My son, if you accept my words and store up my commands within you, turning your ear to wisdom and applying your heart to understanding, and if you look for it as for silver and search for it as hidden treasure, then you will understand the fear of the Lord and find the knowledge of God." Simply stated, God is a conditional God.

The Roots of Leadership

Invariably, any substantive discussion of character will eventually turn to leadership. This is because when someone has achieved or overcome any lengthy adversity or has been placed in leadership, then there is someone observing their actions and behaviors for the purpose of obtaining what they have obtained. Thus, inherent to character development is the title leader and once again I must eliminate a couple of myths.

Most likely you have heard the expression, *a born leader*. This is a myth. I acknowledge that we are born with certain qualities and traits, but until it is developed, then you do not become that thing. For example, a common statement made about a child who takes charge on the playground is that *the child is a born leader*. In reality, the child has been exposed to some form of leadership, whether it is through their parents or teachers or friends. A known assertion is that children mimic the behavior of those to whom they interact and therefore if the predominant interaction is with those who have learned leadership, then the child will adapt to this behavior. Everyone is born with the potential to lead, but the developing process is where things fall short. This is important because the careless use of this expression can have a negative impact on the child that is not assertive or who has yet to be exposed to leaders. If one child is singled out as a born leader and is revered for those qualities, what message is communicated to the other child or children? Potentially, it can say that this *born leader* is better than you are or worse, that you are less than the other child. Even though the words spoken to the child that demonstrates leadership qualities are uplifting, the other child that may hear those words may

The Roots of Leadership

become discouraged. Be careful not to let edification build up one and tear down another.

Another myth associated with leaders is that leaders must be out in front. I often ask this philosophical question to bring understanding to this: Who would call on whom first, the maintenance man or the chief executive officer? If the air conditioner goes out, then the CEO would call the maintenance man. Position does not dictate leadership; leadership dictates position. For example, I was on the softball team in junior high school. After a game at another school, the team had to walk back to our school. We were close to our school, but it did not appear that way. Roughly, there were ten of us and no one knew how to get home except for one person; the problem was nobody wanted to follow him. No one trusted his leadership despite his position; for he was presumed to be a leader in school. Instead everyone turned to me and expressed their confidence in my ability to get them home. I did not have a clue as to how to get home, but I did not trust nor want to follow the other guy either. So I started walking and everyone followed except for the other guy who knew the way; he went to a store. We walked a couple of blocks and then turned left and saw the guy who no one believed in front of us (he had taken a short cut). I was so relieved to see him and while everyone else followed me, I began follow him. I was not popular in school, but I had a reputation for being smart or the guy who could figure things out; this is what made me a leader in the eyes of those who wanted to get home. The other guy, he knew the way, but was a glory hound and therefore was not respected. They followed me, not because I knew how to get them home, but like the maintenance man, I was diligent in responsibilities and therefore considered reliable in other areas as well. A leader does not have to be out in front, but as a leader respects and completes the tasks laid before them then they will be promoted. Additionally, a leader needs to know their position. Before a leader can effectively deal with the nuisances of positions that have no glamour, a leader would have to establish a personal definition of a leader and determine if that definition is consistent with their current behavior. With this end mind, I offer the following discussion and definition of a leader.

Is becoming a leader a conscious choice or is it inherent to the development of the person? First, you need to acknowledge that becoming a leader is not based on what you do but instead is reflective of who you are. Can you decide to become a leader and successfully grow into one? Second, it should be noted that the demonstration of leadership qualities does not implicitly make you a leader. Is leader the title given to someone who embodies certain characteristics? Third, we must understand that the ideals of a leader will remain even when the leader is gone. A leader is one whose imagination knows no boundaries, whose conscience is unlimited and who is progressively selfaware.

Physically, you could be bound, but your imagination allows movement; it may be a bitter, cold day but you can feel the warmth of the sun; in the middle of winter, you can have roses. Your imagination allows you to develop an alternate reality that gives hope. Utilizing the power of the mind to visualize the uncreated worlds of potential that lie within is a key to having a life of fulfillment. Imagine you have all the riches in the world. Imagine you have the character of a proven leader. Imagine yourself educated. Education is being defined as that learning that causes a sense of purpose to be developed; that learning which promotes vision. This vision affords you the freedom to change your circumstances or environment. It allows you to move beyond desperate conditions and live in peace. Though imprisoned, this vision allows you to be free. The strength of your conscience compels you not to use your freedom as a coverup for wrongdoing.

The faculty of recognizing right and wrong in regard to your conduct coupled with a sense that you should act accordingly, is your conscience. Freedom without conscience is like a bone without muscle; you have the

The Roots of Leadership

ability to stand, but not the capability to move. Your conscience, through discipline, allows you to direct your freedom. Freedom says, I am my own person; I make my own decisions; and I can do what I want. A disciplined conscience says, though I am free and belong to no one I make myself vulnerable to all. Discipline allows you to realize that although everything is permissible, not everything is beneficial. As stated earlier, discipline is hard, but those who are trained by it will reap a great harvest as they simultaneously discover who they are.

Imagination allows for you to progress, because your mind is always free; you have peace in the midst of the storm for you can see beyond the storm. Your conscience tempers your freedom; however, it is through discovery of self or selfawareness that freedom truly exists. Accepting that you are an individual created for a specific purpose preempts jealousy and promotes humility. Selfawareness allows you to understand the difference between holding a hand and chaining a soul. On the day that you discover that you failed a major test, or that your best was not good enough, or when every decision you make is wrong, selfawareness allows you to look in the mirror and like whom you see. Selfawareness means that you recognize that being number one does not mean you are out in front. Selfawareness causes you to understand positional leadership; to understand that not everyone can be on top. If everyone were on top, there would be no top. Selfawareness lets you find your place and have peace there. Once you know who you are, it does not matter what you do. Humility comes easily as you understand that leadership is not an external event, but an internal happening. Selfawareness is having knowledge of the essential or specific being of the individual person. A leader is someone who willingly walks the path of selfdiscovery; one who continually gravitates toward the optimal; one who embraces the sun that is covered or hidden by clouds. Before you can stand as a leader, you should choose to strive toward having victory over self. The essence of the personal leader lies within

The Roots of Character

the heart and in this vain, you should now ask yourself: Am I a leader?

Hopefully, the answer was yes; if nothing else, your interest in reading this book suggests that you want to be better than you are through character development; as you travel this path, your leadership will be defined. At a minimum, you will be a leader of self. As such, your leadership is coming, but I dare you to be a great leader! To achieve this greatness, there are few dynamics to leadership that must be understood and applied to your life: servanthood, being an example and making yourself unnecessary. Again, understanding these principles is not enough; these principles require action.

First, is the principle of servanthood, the root word being servant, which is defined as one who expresses submission, recognizance or debt to another. The most significant component to this definition is the word submission. Submission requires humility. Humility is an element that demands a high level of excellence and commitment to be present, whether you are the keynote speaker or the keynote speaker's chauffeur. If servanthood is truly understood, then it does not matter what you do as long as the task is successfully completed. This notion reverts to the definition of submission; to submit is to accept guidance or to follow. This is the point where you realize that there is a purpose, goal or vision greater or more important than you, thus you are intrinsically forced to humble and submit yourself and follow the vision. 2 Chronicles 7:14, says, If my people, who are called by my name would humble themselves and pray and seek my face and turn from their wicked ways, then I will hear from heaven and will forgive their sin and heal their land. Through demonstrated humility and recognition that God is the source and not allowing evil to live in your hearts, God will respond to the cries of His people and turn every evil situation around. We must forget about ourselves and concentrate on the Lord's purpose. A servant, whose focus is on the fulfillment of the cause, and not on self,

The Roots of Leadership

immediately becomes a good follower. This is the underlying meaning to the saying to be a good leader, you have to first become a good follower. Once you become a leader, otherwise referred to as a master of servanthood, you will be looked upon for direction and guidance. You will be expected to be and example.

An example is a representative of a group as a whole or one that serves as a pattern of a specific kind. An example is quite different from a role model. How often have you read about some wellknown celebrity, minister, or sports personality participating in drugs or some other disappointing act, which effectively paralyzes the dreams of some child (or even adults)? This figure was a role model, who in the eyes of most, had succeeded and is looked upon to help develop or encourage young minds. Coming out of a bad neighborhood, overcoming great obstacles, or successfully traveling the road not taken, may make you a role model, but it does not automatically qualify you to be an example. The key difference between a role model and an example is that an example accepts responsibility for the dependency that others invariably place on him. Paul explains it this way in 1 Corinthians 11:1, "Follow my example, as I follow the example of Christ." In other words, if he does not follow or continue to follow Christ, then you are under no obligation to follow him. To continue with the sports analogy, a role model would have an option contract, while an example would sign on for life.

An example does not have the option of changing or stopping; wherever he is, at home, at work, or on vacation it does not matter. The responsibility to his followers remains. A leader who represents a group must always conduct himself or herself appropriately at all times. The issue is not about protecting self; it is about protecting the confidence that others have in you. There exists great dependency between followers and leaders. Hebrews 13:7 reads, "Remember your leaders, who spoke the Word of God to you. Consider the outcome of their way of life and imitate their faith." In this regard, imitate means to adopt

The Roots of Character

your leader's faith until you develop your own faith; this supports the notion that is found in Hebrews 6:1-2, "Let us leave the elementary teachings about Christ and go on to maturity, not laying again the foundation of repentance from acts that lead to death and of faith in God, instruction about baptisms, the laying of hands, the resurrection of the dead and eternal judgment." There should come a point in your walk with God where you no longer have to depend on someone else's faith to get you through; you should grow and reach a level of independence in faith, such that you can believe God in prayer for yourself. This independence allows for prayer partners to be established; now, there are two who can willingly rely on each other for support, while simultaneously seeking God. On a side note, please take notice as to what is considered to be elementary teachings in Hebrews 6:1-2 and work on growing beyond the basics of faith and focus on the deeper things in God.

Nonetheless, the dependency between leaders and followers is sometimes longlasting and potentially selfserving. I am aware of some in leadership who refuse to cut the umbilical cord and continue to be the lifeline between God and His people. This is an unfortunate situation because leadership, if effective, will make itself increasingly unnecessary. This last element, becoming unnecessary rests at the core of leadership and is a byproduct of being an example. Fundamentally, this concept distinguishes between being a motivator and an inspirator. A motivator is an artificial life, a respirator, which causes one to breathe. It is an external force from which the recipient, if separated, would die. A motivated person needs to be hooked up to the motivator in order to be effective. An inspirator is one who breathes life into another, such that the recipient becomes selfsustaining and inherently desires to continue in pursuit of the vision. The parable of the two sons in Matthew 21:28-20 is the perfect example. It reads, "There was a man who has two sons. He went to the first and said, 'Son, go and work today in the vineyard.' 'I will not.' He answered but later

The Roots of Leadership

he changed his mind. The father went to the other son and said the same thing. He answered, 'I will,' but he did not go. Without adding to the Word of God, I have simplified this parable to bring more understanding. Every day this man would wake his sons early in the morning to work in the vineyards. The elder son, in his father's presence, performed his duties with an apparent zeal for the work, but in the father's absence he disrespected and resented the work. The younger son watched his father's diligence. He dreamed of being like him and therefore took great pride in doing his best even when his father was not around. In either scenario, this passage typifies inspiration versus motivation. The elder son needed his father to be near to be effective; he was motivated. The younger son was inspired. This inspiration would allow him to achieve when no one was watching; he would achieve because it became important to him. The father's presence was unnecessary to his younger son because he had inspired him to grab the vision for himself.

This notion of making yourself unnecessary leads to a peculiar question: Is a leader a person? The first thought is that a leader has to be a person, but just like impressions, the first one does not necessarily tell all there is. The expanded definition of a leader is the ideology or conceptual framework, which defines an individual's habits and behaviors that are desired by those who observe them; simply put, this means that a leader is one who does something and leaves an impression that others will embrace and mimic. Although this is a personal preference, the leader that this describes does not have to be a saved, sanctified, prayer warrior setting the world on fire for Jesus; ironically, this leader can be your neighborhood drug dealer or gang leader.

Drug dealers and gang leaders, at times, have more effective recruiting techniques than some evangelists. Please do not misunderstand, I do not condone those behaviors, but leadership is clearly demonstrated by the increasing number of followers. Provoking others to participate in immoral acts is a question of character, not leadership. Per the definition above, when a gang leader is gone (does not matter how, prison or death) there is someone, a disciple, who takes over to lead and follow the path of the former leader. Every leader, good or bad, has someone following them; someone prepared to take the reigns in their absence. The distinguishing factor, between good and bad, is the character of the leader. Either way this boils down to ideology.

Think for a moment about someone you consider a leader. Your thoughts may immediately turn toward what this person does and not physical characteristics; thoughts of strength, integrity, righteousness, prayer life, truthfulness, friendly, successful, etc. Whatever the thought is that makes this person your leader and what you want to obtain will be based on the character of the person. For example, suppose your leader is a minister and this minister embodies everything you want to become in God. He or she loves God and continues to seek Him every day; there is constant prayer, ministry to the sick and elderly, family life is in tact, etc. Simply, imagine this mentor who can teach you all the things you want to know about God, based on their ministry and lifestyle. Now, imagine that you find out that this same minister has committed some grave sin, like stealing, or the thing that usually pops to mind, adultery. Your great leader has just committed adultery; the person to whom you are following has sinned and it is now public knowledge. On the basis of this sin, do you now discount and ignore all the principles that were being taught? Perhaps he does not sin, but dies, do you forget about the teachings that came forth? If you follow the man the human being, then you will fall or die with the man. You must come to a point where no matter how exciting and inspiring someone is the focus stays on God. God should be at your center or the overriding factor to all decisions made.

God says to put your trust in no man and even more so in Jeremiah 17:9, "The heart is deceitful above all things

The Roots of Leadership

and beyond cure. Who can understand it?" Why put so much confidence in the natural when that which you seek is spiritual? Consider this, after meeting someone for the first time and later discussing the person a common statement is, "I can not put my finger on it, but there is something about . . ." Good or bad, this is the spirit bearing witness with another spirit and from that initial encounter character determinations will be made; not necessarily the correct determination, but a determination nonetheless. Character speaks even before someone opens their mouth. This is beyond sizing someone up based on appearance; this is listening with your eyes and spirit. For example, my former barber and I were engaged in a conversation, this is after he had been cutting my hair for sometime. During our talk, I shared with him that I was a disciple of Christ and explained what that means; he then said, "That's it!" Obviously, I asked "What?" He then said that "He noticed a peace about me; a quiet confidence." Prior to that conversation, I was communicating to him about the leader in me. As the Word says "Greater is He that is in me, than he that is in the world".

    It is time to realize that the leader is not who you are following; you are following the principles that are applied in the leader's life. Unfortunately, there is tendency to rely on the person rather than what is in the person. Due to natural limitations established by humanity, people can fail you. Therefore, elevating someone to superficial levels not only sets you up for failure, but potentially causes the leader to become egotistical. We must begin to focus on that which lies within; remember that our bodies are temporary housing for the Spirit of God. As we develop in relationship with God, the Spirit manifests Himself in our lives and our character is developed. It is from this base than we communicate without words. Obviously, I am talking about character and principles of God and not the immoral leader referred to earlier. Through this communication, leaders impart the principles of character that inspire others.

The Roots of Development

All roots need to go through the process of development. Even after maturing to handle its duties or fulfill its purpose, roots continue to grow. This maturity is a process of time and inherently contains trials and tribulations for the purpose of developing the character of the person. The story of Joseph chronicles his maturation and also encompasses many of the nuances of development.

Joseph needed to learn or develop wisdom. In Genesis, chapter 37, the story begins by explaining how Joseph was his father's favorite son because he was born to him in his old age; also, it tells of Joseph's need for wisdom. Joseph's brothers hated him because his father loved him more and treated him accordingly. If you consider normal sibling rivalries and relationships, then Joseph had to have known of this contempt for him. Given that, why would he tell the people who hate him that one day they are going to bow down to him? As we learn from the story, Joseph had plenty to learn and wisdom was paramount. Nonetheless, Joseph told his brothers of the dream that he had, which included his father and mother bowing down to him as well. Joseph also told his father, Israel, these dreams and his father rebuked him, but kept the matter in mind. Part of the correction by Israel was to impart to Joseph wisdom in speech; hence, just because something is true, does not mean that it needs to be told.

The jealousy from his brothers would only worsen by knowing that they were going to bow down to him one day. They hated him, but somehow they had to believe or accept the possibility that what his dream was come true; if they did not believe, then it could have been used as a point of ridicule indicating that Joseph was merely out of his mind.

The Roots of Development

Instead, when they saw Joseph coming toward them from a distance, they said to each other in verse 19, "Come now, let's kill him and throw him into one of these cisterns and say that a ferocious animal devoured him. Then we'll see what comes of his dreams." Remember, many are the plans of man, but the plans of God shall prevail. Reuben, Israel's first born, wanted to rescue Joseph and persuaded his brothers not to kill him but to throw him in the cistern; he was going to rescue him later and take him back to his father. When Joseph had come near, they stripped him of his clothes and threw him into an empty cistern. For perspective, a cistern is a water tank similar to the large tanks that are seen around rural towns; the difference is that cisterns are in the ground. So Joseph was thrown into the cistern. As they sat down to eat their meal, they saw a caravan coming their way and decided to sell Joseph. Specifically, in verses 26 and 27, "Judah said to his brothers, 'What will we gain if we kill our brother and cover up his blood?' Come, let's sell him to the Ishmaelites and not lay our hands on him; after all, he is our brother, our own flesh and blood.' His brothers agreed." Imagine that, they say, "He's our brother don't kill him, just sell him into slavery." Reuben apparently did not want to eat with them and was feeling remorse for Joseph for when he returned to the cistern, Joseph was gone. In hindsight, the Lord must have led Reuben away; otherwise he would not have allowed Joseph to be sold into slavery. Joseph needed to learn how to serve; as his father's favorite, it appears as if he was protected by his father and did not have to work like his brothers; in verse 12, the bible says that Israel sent Joseph to his brothers to check on them and bring him a report as to how they are doing. Hence, Joseph needed to understand servanthood if he was to indeed rule as his dreams indicated. Upon arriving in Egypt, the Ishmaelites sold Joseph to Potiphar, the captain of the guard.

Despite being enslaved, the Lord was with Joseph. Chapter 29, verses 2-5 records, "The Lord was with Joseph and he prospered, (God can prosper you no matter where you are) and lived in the house of his Egyptian master. When his master saw that the Lord was with him and that the Lord gave him success in everything he did, Joseph found favor in his eyes and became his attendant. Potiphar put him in charge of his household, and he entrusted him to his care everything he owned. From the time he put him in charge of his household and of all that he owned, the Lord blesses the household of the Egyptian because of Joseph." Joseph went from servant, to master of servanthood. Although, he was still a slave, he learned and excelled in stewardship, which he would also need to fulfill his purpose in God. The length of time is not stated concerning Joseph's ascension in Potiphar's house, but years had passed. There had to be enough time for Joseph to stop resisting his situation and trust the Lord; he had to have succeeded in his first position as a slave for he was not initially prospering and living in Potiphar's house and it takes time for someone to be trusted with your entire household. This was God's plan and Joseph's development. In addition to service, Joseph needed the time to learn humility, patience, discipline, and many other character principles. Nonetheless, as Joseph was developing internally, he was succeeding externally and after a while his master's wife took notice of him.

She lusted for him and invited the wellbuilt and handsome Joseph to bed. Not only did he refuse, but also explained why this was completely inappropriate. Verse 8 records his response, "With me in charge my master does not concern himself with anything in the house; everything he owns he has entrusted to my care. No one is greater in this house than I am. My master has withheld nothing from me except you, because you are his wife. How then could I do such a wicked thing and sin against God?" Notice he said against God he did not focus on Potiphar. Unfortunately, she pursued him day after day, but he continued to refuse to go to bed with her or even be with her. Yet again, the time period of this process is not documented but this had to be over a period of weeks or months. This is based on an

The Roots of Development

apparent belief that Potiphar's wife had, in that she could seduce him and get what she wanted. Eventually, she set a trap for him.

As recorded in verses 11 and 12 records, "One day he went into the house to attend to his duties, and none of the household servants was inside. She caught him by his cloak and said, 'Come to bed with me!' But he left his cloak in her hand and ran out of the house. This would be her final attempt at seducing him for she had emptied the house and waited for Joseph. I concluded that she was naked and this is what prompted Joseph to run out of the house. There are times to walk away and then there are times to run! Rejection is a tough pill to swallow, but this rejection that she was experiencing caused her to want revenge. Hence, she lied to her husband concerning what had happened and Joseph ended up in jail.

On a side note, one of the most peculiar things about character is how easily it is forgotten. Joseph did nothing except continue to honor his God and his master. Due to Joseph holding on to his integrity, he caused this woman to be hurt and become vindictive. Potiphar responded as any husband would at the thought of someone trying to rape his wife. Therefore, everything that he had known of Joseph left his mind; he was not thinking about how blessed his house was or any favor that he had. There are times when you may be accused of something, an accusation that is in direct contrast to who you are and what you believe. All the evidence may go against you and your character may be forgotten, but hold on to that same integrity. You may experience prison, literally or figuratively, but God will remember you when others do not. Even if Potiphar had taken the time to listen, Joseph's only defense was to call Potiphar's wife a liar. Yes, there are also times when you seemingly have no legitimate defense; this is when the character test really begins. After all, the true measure of a man's character can only be taken when pressure is applied. Nonetheless, it was all part of God's plan for Joseph to go to jail and the Lord continued to be with him there. Joseph's character and leadership were developed while in Potiphar's house and though he was a slave it was a good experience. To use an analogy, Joseph prospered when the economy was booming; he had to learn to prosper in a depression. Regardless of the state of the economy, God is still God; therefore as long as you stay focused on Him and obey His commands you will have success. Joseph was being given the opportunity to succeed when the conditions were not favorable. He gained favor with the warden as described in verses 22 and 23, "So the warden put Joseph in charge of all those held in the prison, and he was made responsible for all that was done there. The warden paid no attention to anything under Joseph's care, because the Lord was with Joseph and gave him success in whatever he did." The warden sounds a lot like Potiphar. The principles Joseph learned while in Potiphar's house were now being applied in prison. Principles do not change based on conditions and if applied properly will create an avenue of favor.

Joseph needed to learn how to succeed in good times (Potiphar's house) and bad times (prison) because of what the Lord was about to do. While in prison, as recorded in Genesis chapter 40, Joseph interpreted the dreams of two men. One would be restored and the other killed. The one who would be restored was a cup bearer to Pharaoh. He was to tell Pharaoh about Joseph to get him out of prison but he forgot. Two years later, after Pharaoh had dreams that could not be interpreted, the cup bearer remembered Joseph. Joseph was brought from the dungeon or prison and taken before Pharaoh. After interpreting the dreams, which related to seven years of feast and seven years of famine, Joseph spoke these words to Pharaoh in Genesis 41:33-36, "And now let Pharaoh look for a discerning and wise man and put him in charge of the land of Egypt. Let Pharaoh appoint commissioners over the land to take a fifth of the harvest of Egypt during the seven years of abundance. They should collect all the food of these good years that are coming and store up grain under the

The Roots of Development

authority of Pharaoh, to be kept in the cities for food. This food should be held in reserve for the country, to be used during the seven years of famine that will come upon Egypt, so that the country may not be ruined by the famine."

There are two things to point out in these passages. First, Joseph applied great wisdom in talking with Pharaoh; he did not say put me in charge, but worded his statements such that only one conclusion could be drawn. None of Pharaoh's wise men could interpret his dreams and therefore the one who could interpret the dream was surely a wise man. Joseph let Pharaoh conclude this on his own; he merely pointed him through wisdom in speech. The second thing is that the skills acquired while in Potiphar's house and prison, taught Joseph about organization and order; thereby, he was able to communicate a plan to Pharaoh to save Egypt from ruin. You should not discount the position that you are in or the storm that you may be experiencing. These conditions are designed for your development. As you go through the phases of development, learn all you can and master every skill, one day these skills may prove to be extremely valuable even though today, it may appear to be a waste. Joseph was put in charge of Pharaoh's palace and in verse 41 Pharaoh said to Joseph, "I hereby put you in charge of the whole land of Egypt." As Governor of Egypt, Joseph's family, inclusive of his father and mother, bowed down to him just like the dream had indicated.

Joseph's life was full of trials, tribulations and turmoil, but it was all part of God's plan. His development or training period would last thirteen years; he was sold into slavery at seventeen and was thirty when he entered the service of Pharaoh. Since he was in prison for two years, this means that he was in Potiphar's house for eleven years. He faithfully served Potiphar for eleven years and in the blink of eye he was sent to prison. Joseph never lost sight of God throughout his experiences and even when thrown in prison he confidently stated to the cup bearer and baker in verse 8a of chapter 40, "Do not interpretations belong to God? Tell me your dreams." A subtle point here is that Joseph needed to be reminded or encouraged about his destiny. The correct interpretation of their dreams would affirm to Joseph about his own dreams in that he would have to be in a position to govern in order for his brothers to bow to him. Never let go of your dreams, God is not a man that He should lie, nor the son of man that He should change His mind. Joseph's development was a roller coaster ride as it relates to the experiences, but in reality was a steady climb of maturity and preparation to fulfill his purpose in God.

Remembering your Roots

Balaam carried on a conversation with his donkey as if this were routine; he was so angry at his donkey's diversions from his chosen path that he failed to realize that the donkey was having a verbal conversation with him. Numbers 22:21-30 records this event. The Lord had told Balaam to go with the princes of Balak who had come to summon Balaam; this was the second request, the first was rejected. Balaam arose in the morning and went with the princes of Moab, but God was angry with Balaam when he went and the Angel of the Lord stood in the road to oppose him.

To put this in context, God's anger with Balaam was based on the attitude of Balaam's heart. Balaam was a greedy prophet and was offered a fee to curse the Israelites; instead of rejecting the offer, he told them to wait until he received an answer from the Lord. Waiting on an answer from the Lord is a good thing, but Balaam's motivation was greed. The first time Balak's men had come to Balaam, they offered him a fee to curse the Israelites. Although Balaam rejected the offer, in his heart he strongly considered it. By telling Balak's men to wait for an answer, Balaam was stalling so he could figure out how he could possibly get the money. Ultimately, he submitted and obeyed the Lord, but to the Lord it was as if he had taken the money. His actions were indicative of his evil heart and God was going to kill him. Hence, the Angel of the Lord stood in the road with a sword in His hand.

During this time the donkey demonstrated loyalty to her master. In verses 23-28 the bible records the loyalty of a servant to her master. It reads, "When the donkey saw the Angel of the Lord standing in the road with a drawn sword in His hand, she turned off the road into a field. Balaam beat her to get her back on the road. Then the Angel of the Lord stood in a narrow path between two vineyards, with walls on both sides. When the donkey saw the Angel of the Lord, she pressed close to the wall, crushing Balaam's foot against it. So he beat her again. Then the Angel of the Lord moved on ahead and stood in a narrow place where there was no room to turn, either to the right or to the left. When the donkey saw the Angel of the Lord, she lay down under Balaam, and he was angry and beat her with his staff." This epitomizes servanthood because the donkey was acting in the best interest of her master, to the point of saving his life, and the master rewarded her with a beating. The servant saw what the master did not and was chastised for seemingly going against the direction of the master.

Then in verses 28-30, "The Lord opened the donkey's mouth, and she said to Balaam, "What have I done to you to make you beat me these three times?" Balaam answered the donkey, "You have made a fool of me! If I had a sword in my hand, I would kill you right now." The donkey said to Balaam, "Am I not your own donkey, which you have always ridden, to this day? Have I been in the habit of doing this to you?" In other words the donkey said to Balaam, "Do you not know my character?" The donkey was reminding her master of her character and was prompting Balaam to consider it, when evaluating her behavior. The servant said to the master "Let how I have served you count for something!" If Balaam had a sword, he would have killed his donkey; ironically, the donkey's actions were to keep Balaam from being killed by the sword. Flipping back to the story of Joseph, were it not God's plan, Joseph would have communicated to Potiphar the same message of remember my character.

Unfortunately, character appears to be the missing link. Often there is a wide gap or disconnect between what is preached in the pulpit on Sunday mornings and the habits and attitudes demonstrated the rest of the week or outside the pulpit. This is not a criticism of preachers

Remembering your Roots

or teachers and I do recognize the higher standard to which they are held, but James 3:1-3 does, to some degree, validate this higher standard. It reads, "Not many of you should presume to be teachers, my brothers, because you know that we who teach will be judged more strictly. We all stumble in many ways. If anyone is never at fault in what he says, he is a perfect man, able to keep his whole body in check." This means that the words that come out of your mouth are the same words that will be used to validate or invalidate your character as a leader. No one is perfect, but if you understand and can teach the oracles of God then the predominant actions you take should line up with the Word of God. In a nutshell, there should be consistency in action whether you are in the church or stuck in traffic.

As you seek God and adapt your lives to the persona of Jesus Christ, you will be transformed in your inward parts; a transformation that will be revealed as pressure is applied to your daily walk. This development of your character will provoke an even greater hunger and thirst for God. There is an ever increasing reverence for God as you begin to know Him more. You actually begin to discover your place in Him. As stated in I Peter 2:9-10, "You are a chosen people, a royal priesthood, a holy nation, a people belonging to God, that you may declare the praises of Him who called you out of darkness into His wonderful light. Once you were not a people, but now you are the people of God; once you had not received mercy, but now you have received mercy." This is who you are in God, a child of royalty. In your reflection you should see the color purple. You are a child of the King!

There is no denying who you are in the Lord and even if you were to try, denial does not change the truth. 1 Corinthians 12:15-16 says, "If the foot should say, 'Because I am not a hand, I do not belong to the body,' it would not for that reason cease to be a part of the body. And if the ear should say, 'Because I am not an eye, I do not belong to the body,' it would not for that reason cease to

The Roots of Character

be a part of the body. You are who you are because God made you that way. Being tall does not mean you should play basketball, any more than being short makes you a jockey; God created you with those attributes not to align with society's view of what you should do or become, but to fulfill His purpose. Once you embrace who God is, it is a lot easier to progress toward His character. One of the main components to this progress is humility.

David's heart was so full of God that he wanted to build God a house for the Ark of the Covenant. David shared his heart with the Prophet Nathan, who later that night received the Word of God for David. Nathan shared the Word with David and then in verse 16 of 1 Chronicles David said to the Lord, "Who am I, O Lord God, and what is my family, that you have brought me this far?" David was expressing total humility to God for the awesomeness of who He is and for the promises of the future bestowed upon him. He continues to honor and reverence the Lord. Verse 20 says, "There is no one like you, O Lord, and there is no God but you, as we have heard with our own ears." This holy reverence expresses David's humility and complete submission to God. Beyond that, David knew God, but also knew who he was in God. We must reach a place of understanding about God just as David did.

However, your overall attitude should be the same as that of Jesus Christ. Philippians 2:6-11 describes this attitude: "Who, being in very nature God, did not consider equality with God something to be grasped, but made Himself nothing, taking the very nature of a servant, being made in human likeness. And being found in appearance as a man, He humbled Himself and became obedient to death, even death on a cross! Therefore, God exalted Him to the highest place and gave Him the Name that is above every name, that at the Name of Jesus every knee should bow, in heaven and on earth and under the earth and every tongue confess that Jesus Christ is Lord, to the glory of the God the Father." Jesus did not hold on to His position but instead let it go and became human; Jesus separated from Himself

Remembering your Roots

and entered into the human body. At this point being found in appearance as man, He humbled Himself. Jesus was God and decided to become man; when Jesus left the earth, He sent the Holy Spirit to come and comfort us until His return. Since you have God, through the Holy Spirit, you too must humble yourself. As you humble yourself and continue to seek God, then you will be led by the Spirit of the Lord and reflect the character of Him who is inside of you. As stated earlier, pressure brings out what is inside and since you have the Holy Spirit, there is no need to fear tests, trials, storms and especially people. Romans 8:5 says, "Those who live according to the sinful nature have their minds set on what that nature desires; but those who live in accordance with the Spirit have their minds set on what the Spirit desires." To be led by the Spirit you have to connect with the Spirit. "For this Spirit will put to death the misdeeds of the body and those who are led by the Spirit are the sons of God (Romans 8:14)".

In all this, you have to remember your roots and that you are rooted in Christ. There are times when you may not understand everything that is happening to or around you, but always hold on to the fact that you are more than a conqueror. Furthermore, even if you should allow your humanity to show more than the Spirit that lies within you, let these words from Romans 8:38-39 minister to you: "For I am convinced that neither death nor life, neither angels nor demons, neither the present nor the future, nor any powers, neither height nor depth, nor anything else in all creation, will be able to separate you from the love of God that is in Christ Jesus our Lord." It is comforting to know that God is always with you.

The realization that God will never leave, nor forsake you will cause you to venture into unchartered faith and Christ like character. This is what Daniel had obtained. The story of Daniel and the lion's den is known beyond Christian circles, but the magnificence of this story tells of character and is found in chapter 6 in the Book of Daniel. Daniel was one of three administrators, but he distinguished himself from the others because of his exceptional qualities. He was complete with discipline in the carrying on of his work. This demonstrated excellence caused the king to want to promote Daniel to govern the kingdom. The other administrators were jealous of Daniel and tried to find fault with him, but were unable to do so. Daniel was trustworthy and was neither negligent nor corrupt; he was a faithful and committed man, who loved and trusted God. The other administrators and those they were over, the Satraps, knew of Daniel's reverence for the Lord and concluded that unless they use this against him, they would never find fault against him. This is comparable to unsaved or unchurched people quoting scriptures to bring conviction to someone who is saved. They went to the king and eventually convinced him to decree that everyone should only bow to him for the next thirty days. According to the law, a decree can not be changed not even by the king. Since they knew of Daniel's conviction, they knew he would not honor the king's decree and therefore would have a basis from which to accuse him. In verse 10, after "Daniel had learned of the decree had been published, he went home to his upstairs room where the windows opened toward Jerusalem. Three times a day he got down on his knees and prayed, giving thanks to his God, just as he had done before." Daniel had a disciplined lifestyle and no decree was going to stop him from praying to God. Not only did he continue to pray to God, but he also prayed where everyone could see him; he was not openly defying the king, he was openly praying to God. This is why it does not matter what the law says about prayer in schools; if you have a disciplined prayer life, then you are going to pray to God regardless of the law. This is not rebellion, this is submitting to a higher authority; besides, this law relates to schools promoting prayer, not whether or not an individual can pray.

Nonetheless, the administrators and satraps, as a group, went to Daniel's home and found him praying and asking God for help. They told the king and Daniel was

Remembering your Roots

eventually thrown into the lion's den. Although the king did not want to do this, he had to obey the edict. As we know, Daniel was thrown into the lion's den and an angel had come to shut the mouths of the lions. Daniel was not hurt and all his accusers, their wives and children, were thrown into the lion's den. When Daniel was in the window praying, one of the things he prayed for was help that he received from the angel. Daniel's friends, Shadrach, Meshach and Abednego, had the same experience. They were thrown into a furnace because they maintained the integrity of their relationship with God and refused to bow down to other Gods. They told the king that God is able to save them, but even if He does not, they were not going to bow to these other gods. Daniel, Shadrach, Meshach and Abednego had the Spirit of the Lord in them and allowed this Spirit to manifest in their lives. They remembered who they were in God and regardless of the circumstance would not be moved.

Another example of remembering your roots is found in the Book of Esther. Esther, who was beautiful and lovely, was raised by her cousin Mordecai upon the death of her parents. Mordecai and Esther were Jewish exiles from the tribe of Benjamin. By way of summary, the king was persuaded to rid himself of the queen because she disobeyed his request. Through an extensive selection process, Esther was chosen to be the new queen. Now, Haman was promoted by the king to a seat higher than all his other officials; the king had also commanded that all royal officials should kneel down and pay honor to Haman. Mordecai refused and Haman had become so angry that he not only wanted to kill Mordecai, but all Jews throughout the whole kingdom. Haman convinced the king and the ensuing decree read that all Jews were to be killed on the thirteenth day of the twelfth month. Mordecai learned of this and persuaded Esther to help.

During this entire process, Esther had never revealed her nationality, per the instructions of her cousin. However, she was Jewish and therefore would be

The Roots of Character

impacted by the decree. Mordecai asked Esther to help her people. However, Esther was the queen of the most powerful kingdom and was most likely enjoying her position. Mordecai's request was met with an excuse. Obviously, she had not fully appreciated the gravity of the situation since she was now the queen. Esther told Mordecai that anyone who approaches the king without being summoned would be put to death. Mordecai's response as recorded in Esther 4:13-14, "Do not think that because you are in the king's house you alone of all the Jews will escape. For if you remain silent at this time, relief and deliverance for the Jews will arise from another place, but you and your father's family will perish. And who knows but that you have come to royal position for such a time as this?" These words from Mordecai caused Esther to remember her roots. Esther, who had been depending on Mordecai to impart wisdom to her, began to impart wisdom of her own. She requested for all the Jews to fast for three days and nights while she and her maids did the same. Afterwards, even though it is against the law, she would go to the king. "And if I perish, I perish." she said.

Esther was demonstrating great character; she was putting herself in harms way to save the Jews. On the third day of the fast, Esther entered the inner court of the palace and the king welcomed her. However, she used wisdom in asking for her people to be saved; she says in chapter 7, verse 3, "If I have found favor with you, O king, and if it pleases your majesty, grant me my life—this is my petition. And spare my people—this is my request." Keep in mind that until this point the king did not know she was Jewish; Esther was able to tell him who she was and save her life and the lives of her people at the same time. Furthermore, she did it with such grace and wisdom that it resulted in the death of Haman, the enemy of her people.

She needed prompting, but Esther realized that it was not in God's plan to have the Jews annihilated and that if she did nothing, God would spare them through some other means. This prompting reminded Esther of

Remembering your Roots

her humble beginnings and that God was in charge. The statement made by Mordecai, "For such a time as this," is one that speaks to the purpose behind our development. God develops our character to carry out His purposes and plans for His people. If you become so enthralled with your position, then you may begin to make excuses for not doing what you were prepared to do. God is not a respecter of persons and always has a ram in the bush. Your character is reflected as you are called to fulfill your purpose and as a prerequisite, you will be tested.

The final point on remembering your roots relates to this test. Matthew 20:1-16, the parable of the workers in the vineyard is told. In summary, early in the morning, several workers were hired by a landowner to work is his vineyard. The agreement made was one denarius (a small Roman coin made of silver) for a day's work. Throughout the day, specifically on the third, sixth, ninth and eleventh hours, the landowner went out to the marketplace and hired more workers; he agreed to pay them what was right. At the end of the day, the landowner gave instructions to his foreman to pay the workers their wages. The foreman paid those who worked for the least amount of time first. He paid them one denarius. On the basis of what they were paid, those who had worked all day expected to receive more but they received one denarius as well. Verse 11 says that "When they received it, they began to grumble against the landowner." They felt as though it was wrong for those who had worked all day to receive the same pay as those who worked for one hour. Verse 13 records the landowner's response, "Didn't you agree to work for a denarius?" In other words, you were hired to do a job for a day and agreed to be paid a day's wages; you did the job and I paid you accordingly. We had an agreement and I honored it. There is a tendency to compare the labor of one to another and just like in the parable the comparison is invalid. The early morning workers thought they were receiving a great blessing to receive one denarius and would have gone home quite content had they not known the wages of those who

The Roots of Character

worked one hour. This is why it is good for coworkers not to know another's salary. For example, during the season of annual increases, I received an increase that I felt was beneath my value to the company; in my frustration with the amount I discussed it with a fellow employee. Later when she received her increase it was comparable to mine and she was satisfied, until I told her I challenged my increase and received more.

She felt as though she were my professional equal and was content as long as I was under valued; when she found out that I was validated everything changed. This is when I discovered what not to talk about in the office. As for the frustrated vineyard workers, they failed the character test to their own detriment. This grumbling, most likely, would cause the landowner not to hire them the next day or any other day. The lesson in this is that your word is all you have; hence, if you have accepted a job and agreed to a certain pay, you are bound by your own words and actions concerning that job. The fact that someone else was blessed outside of your agreement should not have a bearing on you or your performance. Romans 12:2 says, "Do not conform any longer to the pattern of this world, but be transformed by the renewing of your mind. Then you will be able to test and approve what God's will is—His good, pleasing and perfect will." God is a God of abundance and as a final thought, always remember your roots.

The Beginning

A strong, positive character is not automatic; it includes the natural element of time. Character, like leadership, needs to be developed. I deliberately pull in the concept of leadership here because of the false expression, a *born leader*. Leaders possess the traits of leadership at birth; however, the manifestation occurs after proper development. The earlier a child exhibits leadership qualities there is a blind tendency to say that the child was born that way, rather than apply legitimacy to parents, teachers, mentors, etc. Likewise, men and women of character need to be developed through the same standards of legitimacy; standards that encompass time. For example, Job was a righteous man who feared God and shunned evil. Job did his best to personally honor God and to keep his children before the Lord. He even sacrificed burnt offerings on their behalf in the event they sinned (Job 1:1-5). Job had matured to a wise, old man and developed in relationship with and possessed a deep understanding of who God is.

On the basis of Job's righteousness in God, the devil expressed his boredom to God with being able to successfully roam ". . . through the earth and going back and forth it." This statement by the devil meant that he could easily do whatever he wanted with God's people. To Satan's statement of contempt, the Lord responded, "Have you considered my servant Job?" Wow, what a testament to Job's character; the Lord God is effectively bragging on Job's integrity and ability to stay connected to Him. At the end of this discourse God permitted the devil to test Job as he wanted; everything was fair game with the restriction, he could not take his life. However, the devil is anything but fair when coming after you.

The Roots of Character

First, all of Job's oxen were stolen and all but one of his men were killed; this one had the responsibility to go tell Job of his lost; then fire fell from the sky and killed all his sheep and servants except one; this one also had the responsibility to tell Job of his lost; the same happened for his camels and worse of all, his sons and daughters were also killed. If that were not enough, be mindful, all of this was the first test; Job was severely weakened and hurting, but did not sin.

On another day, Satan came before the Lord with other angels and expressed his boredom yet again. This time Satan was more duplicitous than bored; to his statement the Lord again expressed confidence in Job and gave permission for Satan to touch his skin, but still not his life. So the second test afflicted Job flesh so that he could turn away from God. The bible records in Job 2:7, that Job was afflicted with painful sores from the soles of his feet to the top of his head. This literally means that he could not position himself for any comfort. Imagine him lying on the sores as gently as possible, but then gravity caused his weight to burst blisters underneath him; simultaneously, the other painful sores are still hurting and increasing in irritation from his cover or blanket. As he agonized over his physical condition Job, looking for some ounce of comfort, took a piece of broken pottery and scrapped himself with it as he sat among the ashes (Job 2:8). Keep in mind, this is after he has lost his family; there was no time to mourn because the pain never ended. Again, the devil uses pain and discomfort to try to cause the people of God to turn away from God. The devil failed in his attempt to get Job to curse God. Yet, the brutal agony of this caused Job's wife to encourage him to "Curse God and die!" Yet, Job merely called his wife foolish and maintained his integrity toward God, i.e., he still did not sin. After this came the greatest test of all . . . his friends.

Initially, Job friends were supportive and merely troubled by his agony and pain. They sat with Him seven days and nights never speaking a word for they saw how

The Beginning

great his suffering was. As time went on, his friends tried to explain and reason why these things were happening to him. In their minds this action had to be the result of some sin that Job had committed; somehow, Job was responsible for this devastation that had occurred in his life. Even to the point where he was literally accused of being wicked as a young man. That's right, wicked! The man whom God selected to be tested by the devil was described as a wicked man. His friend said that Job demanded money from his brothers without cause; he stripped men of their clothing, leaving them naked and ashamed. He gave no water to the weary and no food to the hungry. He sent widows away empty handed and broke the strength of the fatherless (Job 22:4-9). This analysis of character was used by Job's friend as the basis to explain the current turmoil in his life. What Job and his friends failed to understand was that God had permitted all this to occur because he believed in Job. Unfortunately, those who knew you before you became a servant of God will quickly remind you of who you use to be or offer misguided explanations for things that are beyond their reach. This alludes to what Jesus observed when He said that "A prophet is of no honor in his home town." If your position or relationship with God can be reduced to the *old self* then your message of redemption can be rejected as simple bantering or if someone refuses to see the change and growth in you, then whomever may not have to come to grips with the stagnation or nondevelopment in their own lives. Nonetheless, Job was trusted by God to be a man of integrity and this trust was so great that God granted the devil permission to challenge Job in his faith. All of Job's losses were intended to cause him to turn his back on God. Now, remember, the devil had permission to touch everything except Job's life and the sparing of Job's life included his wife. This not only shows that God honors the marital covenant, but also that, in marriage, man and woman become one flesh. To kill Job's wife would be to kill Job because of their oneness and the devil was restricted from touching his life. Even though

The Roots of Character

she, out of her own pain and anguish, told him to curse God and die, she was still under the covenant; besides, Job's wife was not the one being tested, Job was.

The tests that Job experienced took him on an emotional and physical whirlwind. Throughout his ordeal, though he questioned, argued and even complained to God about his sufferings, he never lost sight of nor abandoned God. Job's statement in Job 13:15 epitomize his commitment and conviction; he says, "Though He slay me, yet will I serve Him." Effectively, Job verbalized what he had already done in his spirit; he drew a line in the sand and was not going to let any circumstances cause him to cross. Thus, instead of letting his frustration and difficulties control him, he took control of them not let the negativity of his friends be borne in him. Although Job may have breached the area of pride and became self righteous as he began to justify his actions; to which he was aptly corrected, first by Elihu then by God himself. In the end, Job received a double portion; all that he had lost was received back in abundance; additionally, he had to pray for his friends so that God would not deal with them according to their folly. Nonetheless, Job never lost the integrity of his relationship with God; he remained loyal and faithful as he took ownership of the pain he was experiencing. As I state in the last line of a stanza: Never feel sorry for a man who owns the pain!

Instinctively, the emphasis is directed toward the pain; the operative term in that statement is actually own. When someone owns something they can decide the fate of that thing. If a car, it can be sold; if a house, it can be a refuge; if pain, it can be released. If someone has ownership of pain then you do not have to feel sorry for them; instead help them let go of the pain. Sometimes, to let go you actually have to fully embrace the situation. Invariably, as a part of our humanity, we will experience some kind of hurt; a hurt that causes lasting pain; a pain that if allowed can tie you up in chains. Instead of the freedom of the Lord, you

The Beginning

may be bound. On this subject I wrote the following poem titled *There's No Chain*:

> The mind does not move because of what it believes
> The man does not step because of what he sees
> You may be naked and unashamed
> But your strength does not lift me up
>
> I want you to know my destiny
> Liberty comes because I am free
> I wish you could understand
> But not if I have to die in the process
>
> There's plenty wrong and you're lost in dependence
> Sometimes you're troubled and it makes sense
> Indifference is a decision
> You know Perfection that's why you're alive
>
> Don't abuse the officer and gentle-man
> Life is yours to embrace, if you think you can
> Appreciate the distance traveled
> Even if it's only in your imagination
>
> It's not what's there
> But it's what you believe
> If you look down you may discover
> There's no chain!

This last chapter is the beginning of the rest of your life; a life that you can choose to be marred by past experiences or one that is brightened by the realization that you can do all things through Christ Jesus who strengthens you. The poem is about this decision making process and the defining or redefining of your character. It says that you should not have your dependency or life tied to man and not to mistreat yourself. However, the most important thing is that no matter how great a past event was, it does not have to chain you down. If you made a mistake, learn from it, if necessary ask for forgiveness, and move on. There is nothing that happened in the past that can be undone; you can only learn from it so you do repeat the same mistake. This understanding is a process; a process that begins with the right decision. For the unsaved, this right decision is to accept Jesus Christ as your Lord and Savior. This is one of the most magnificent things that will ever happen to you. In the blink of an eye, you will be transformed and can begin to live your life as Christ would have you live. The prayer is: Father God, I confess my sins and realized that I do not want to live my life without you. I believe you came, died and rose again for my sins and now I ask that you enter my heart. In Jesus' name, I pray. Amen. For those of you, who prayed this prayer, welcome to the family. For the saved, the right decision is to seek after God's character with your whole heart.

Whether you had two decisions to make or only one, your future in God is greater than yesterday. As you continue to seek after God's heart and develop a personal relationship with Him, your character and leadership will be noticed. Just because your leadership is recognized does not mean that it will be accepted or even wanted. You will have your supporters and those who doubt your position as God's friend. Ironically, if your leadership is recognized, then doubt will still be applied to the legitimacy of your relationship with God. This is why you should not live your life looking for horizontal affirmations. God affirms those who faithfully serve Him through increased anointing. Notwithstanding, lack of acceptance does not mean you should revert to a former state of being; it means that you are doing the right thing and are gravitating toward God.

A developed character or leadership does not mean perfection; it only means that you have overcome many of the setbacks or roadblocks that are affecting others. Proof of your leadership does not happen when you are right; it is made clear when you are wrong. People who have developed their character seek to maintain the integrity of their relationship with God. However, these same people

The Beginning

must realize that everyone is not at the same level and that their 'higher' level only means that they have a different view. From the other person's standpoint, behavior that you may describe as immature makes perfect sense. You have to realize that despite how much you know, there is still so much that you do not know. As children of God, we know in part and understand in part; when Jesus returns, then we will know all. Also, as a developed leader, you have to produce for God; otherwise, according to Matthew 3:10, "The ax is at the root of the tree."

This book started with roots and trees and it is appropriate that it would end with the same. It takes up to thirty years for some trees to mature; trees, or its derivatives, are used in homes, boats, buildings, etc. Additionally, trees provide shade to anyone who wants it and can be useful in the preparing of food for the nourishment of our bodies. Ironically and perhaps most appropriately, Jesus started his ministry at thirty and was a carpenter. He spent His developmental years learning to master the use of trees and ultimately, Jesus saved humanity through the roots.

Through the application of the Word of God and other material that simplifies or explains the Word, you will be blessed. Psalms 1:1-3 plainly states, "Blessed is the man who does not walk in the counsel of the wicked or stand in the way of sinners or sit in the seat of mockers. But his delight is in the law of the Lord, and on his law he meditates day and night. He is like a tree planted by the streams of water, which yields its fruit in season and whose leaf does not wither. Whatever he does prospers."

May the grace of the Lord Jesus Christ keep you until you are firmly rooted in Him; Grace to all who love our Lord Jesus and seek him an undying love. Finally, brothers and sisters in Christ, aim for perfection, be of one mind and live in peace. God bless.

Character Development Exercises

Introduction

I am hopeful that you have not grown weary of trees as I am starting this character development section off with another discussion on trees but this time, as everything comes together, you will appreciate the depth and power of this metaphor. A tree, specifically, the apple tree is a magnificent creation and serves as the perfect cornerstone upon which we will continue to build and develop our character. The apple tree is used merely as an example; overall, trees have a wide variety of uses, but for now, this writing will highlight the apple tree.

Usually when thinking about apple trees the first thought is about apples. Now, apples can be eaten right off the tree or used to make apple sauce, apple juice, apple pie, apple butter, dumplings, candy, pastry, cider, wine etc. Assuming that you have eaten something derived from an apple (or perhaps the fruit from another fruit tree), have you ever taken a moment to consider the tree itself or the process undergone to produce that fruit? Speaking as a novice, the process is a seed that is properly planted and watered will sprout a few leaves; it will continue to grow into what will only resemble a tree; in meaningful and appropriate time, it will mature into a full tree and eventually produce fruit. The nutrients that eventually produce the fruit come through the roots from the soil that is enriched by the sun, water, fertilizer, etc. These nutrients pass through the wood, out to the branches and eventually grow into wonderful, nutritious treats for you.

Additionally, apple trees are a beautiful addition to any landscape, providing shade, a delicious harvest and great eye appeal as they flower; apples trees are also used in

Introduction

cooking (apple wood chips for barbecue), have a medicinal benefit based on the acids in the fruit; even apple cider vinegar helps to relieve sinus infections, sore throats, high cholesterol to name a few. In fact, my wife's friend drinks it regularly to assist in breaking down fat and to get healthier. Nutritionally, apples contain a lot of healthy ingredients that I have trouble pronouncing, like phloridzin; nonetheless, this is one of many nutrients that support the heart and benefit the skin. Apples have antifungal and antiseptic properties that also help the physical body remain healthy. Beyond the body, the wood from the apple tree, which is dense, can be used in to produce furniture, doors etc. From a single seed, many of life's pleasures are derived; this sacrificial seed must completely give of itself in order carry out its purpose.

The apple seed can not long to be a peach, orange or banana; it must remain true to its nature and purpose. This seed is dependent upon the environment in which it is placed to meet its unique needs for growth and development. Apples trees can grow almost anywhere, but do not do well in tropical areas; bananas need a tropical region to excel. Neither the apple, nor the banana can thrive outside of its environment. Hopefully, the value of this apple tree metaphor as it relates to your character and the development thereof is clear. Notwithstanding, a tree or even its seed operates or functions according to how it is made; there is no thought or pretense, no decisions to ponder or second guessing; no *I am not going to grow an apple because I do not want whomever to have any* ; a tree fulfills its purpose on the basis of what it is. In contrast, we, human beings, have a choice to make about fulfillment and accomplishment; we have to decide to be different, to be better and to reach our potential in God and in life.

Years ago, a student of mine asked me this question relative to the leadership information that I was teaching and per her observation *living*, "How do you know this stuff?" or "How did you get to this point?" After my obvious deflection of her insinuation, I told her that one day I just decided that I was better than I had been and no longer to wanted to be on the fence; the reality is that God was pulling me into Himself and there is no way the light of God can be encompassed in darkness. No, I was not evil, but I was not righteous either. The more I learned about God and the great men and women of the bible, the more I embraced the idea that I needed to change. I believe it is with a similar notion that led you to this book and these exercises. As with any development process, there is an obvious need to be completely honest and open with yourself; these exercises will only produce for you and lead you down the path of character development if you allow the real you to become evident; this is your life, your growth and most of all, your decision.

The first thing you will do is to take a good look at who you are or who you believe you are; simultaneously, you can detail who you want to be, in other words, write your vision for self development. Again, take your time, be truthful and enjoy this journey of selfdiscovery and development.

1. As you are today, what could God build with you?

Current Assessment:
_____
_____
_____
_____

Vision:
_____
_____
_____
_____

Introduction

2. If someone needed to be loved, could God count on you to love them without condition?

Current Assessment:
_____
_____
_____
_____

Vision:
_____
_____
_____
_____

3. Do you think about tomorrow?

Current Assessment:
_____
_____
_____
_____

Vision:
_____
_____
_____
_____

4. If you could change something from your past, would you?

Current Assessment:
_____
_____
_____
_____

Vision:
_____
_____
_____

5. Do you give when you feel the urge to give?

Current Assessment:
_____
_____
_____

Vision:
_____
_____
_____

6. How does your faith work for you?

Current Assessment:
_____
_____
_____

Vision:
_____
_____
_____

Introduction

7. Would you follow your own advice?

Current Assessment:
_____
_____
_____
_____

Vision:
_____
_____
_____
_____

8. If you were tired, would you start something that you did not want to do but that needed to be done?

Current Assessment:
_____
_____
_____
_____

Vision:
_____
_____
_____
_____

9. What kind of impact are you having on someone's life?

Current Assessment:
_____
_____
_____
_____

Vision:
_____
_____
_____

10. What are you afraid of?

Current Assessment:
_____
_____
_____
_____

Vision:
_____
_____
_____

11. What do you want to be said of you at your funeral?

Current Assessment:
_____
_____
_____
_____

Vision:
_____
_____
_____

Introduction

12. Why were you created? What do you want to do with your life?

Current Assessment:
_____
_____
_____
_____

Vision:
_____
_____
_____
_____

Last question in this first group: How would being a person of noble character help you fulfill your purpose?

_____
_____
_____
_____

Now, as you have gone through this introduction into you, chances are there are some thing that you liked and more things that you do not like. It is really important to focus in on the documented vision as oppose to what you are or may be lacking. Besides, all of this is about growth; remember that the seed had to die to self in order to produce.

The Roots of Character

MEMORY VERSES

1 Corinthians 12:11—All these are the work of one and the same Spirit, and he gives them to each one, just as he determines.

1 Timothy 3:1—Here is a trustworthy saying: If anyone sets his heart on being an overseer, he desires a noble task.

Luke 17:21b—because the kingdom of God is within you.

Isaiah 61:7a—Instead of their shame my people will receive a double portion, and instead of disgrace they will rejoice in their inheritance;

Building for Character

Intimacy is purposeful and is literally at the core of God's desire for us. On the sixth day, this desire for man manifested and intimacy was borne; some time later, this same intimacy, this uninhibited fellowship with God was broken and traded for man's own desire. From the beginning, God's intent and desire was to have communion with man and it remains to this day. This intimate relationship is as much a part of your character as anything. Always remember that the development of your character requires time alone with God for it is in this interaction that you will really discover you are.

1. God has been described many ways, how do you see God?
   _____
   _____
   _____
   _____

2. A tent is a place of separation that allows for intimate connection and communion with God; do you have a tent? Describe it.
   _____
   _____
   _____
   _____

3. How often or how much time do you spend in your tent?
   _____
   _____
   _____
   _____

The Roots of Character

4. What is the tangible evidence that you have been spending time with God?
___
___
___

5. Do you have difficulty being transparent or expressive about you private thoughts? Do you realize that God already knows?
___
___
___

6. Has God ever asked more of your time (woke you up in the middle of the night, not allow you to sleep, an unexpected message for you to read, etc?) How did you respond?
___
___
___

7. Since reading adds depth to your character, when was the last time you read a book and what did you learn from this reading?
___
___
___

8. How much time do you spend in prayer? Why?
___
___
___

Building for Character

9. When was the last time you earnestly prayed for someone else? Describe how you felt afterwards?
___
___
___
___

10. The bible says that we are to have dominion over all the earth and yet, most large animals are stronger and faster than humans; given this, how are we to have dominion?
___
___
___
___

11. Can God trust you with His Word? Why?
___
___
___
___

12. Since God is all powerful and all knowing, why is it necessary for you to pray?
___
___
___
___

MEMORY VERSES

Psalms 27:1a—Unless the Lord builds the house, its builders labor in vain.

1 Corinthians 14:12—So it is with you. Since you are eager to have spiritual gifts, try to excel in gifts that build up the church.

1 Thessalonians 5:11—Therefore encourage one another and build each other up, just as in fact you are doing.

1 Corinthians 3:10—By the grace God has given me, I laid a foundation as an expert builder, and someone else is building on it. But each one should be careful how he builds.

The Roots of Love

1 Corinthians 13:4-8a reads love is patient, love is kind. It does not envy, it does not boast, it is not proud. It is not rude, it is not selfseeking, it is not easily angered, and it keeps no record of wrongs. Love does not delight in evil but rejoices with the truth. It always protects, always trusts, always hopes, and always perseveres. Love never fails.

1. Accepting the above as the definition of love, do you know how to love? Why or why not?

2. Have you ever been impatient or unkind to someone you would say you love? Why?

3. How do you prove your love? Do you feel as though you need to prove you love? Why or Why not?

The Roots of Character

4. Name an occasion where someone has sacrificially loved you. What were the circumstances? How did you feel?
　
　
　
　

5. Have you ever created that feeling in someone else? How did that make you feel? Why?
　
　
　
　

6. Do you need credit or recognition for acts of love performed by you? Why or why not?
　
　
　
　

7. To whom do you compare yourself? Why?
　
　
　
　

8. Despite the things that may have happened to you, do you still have hope for a better life? Why?

The Roots of Love

9. After a significant amount of time has passed, have you ever reminded someone of a hurt or wrong he or she did to you? Why?
_____
_____
_____
_____

10. Are you secretly envious or jealous of someone? Why?
_____
_____
_____
_____

11. How do you show the love of Jesus Christ?
_____
_____
_____
_____

12. What is your personal definition of love?
_____
_____
_____
_____

MEMORY VERSES

1 John 4:16—And so we know and rely on the love God has for us. God is love. Whoever lives in love lives in God, and God in him.

John 15:13—Greater love has no one than this, that he lay his life down for his friends.

1 Corinthians 13:13—And now these things remain: faith, hope and love. But the greatest of these is love.

The Roots of Vision

All things are created twice, first in the mind, and then there is the manifestation. If it stays in your mind, then you have not established it as a vision. It should not be a surprise that between the first citing and second coming is where the depth and truthfulness of a vision lies. From idea to manifestation can be a lengthy process of which your unwavering commitment is required. If you believe that you have a vision that will make a difference in your life and the lives of those to whom you come in contact, then it should be pursued accordingly.

1. Imagine yourself sitting comfortably and resting; you close your eyes and lean your head back and begin to see your future; what do you see?
___
___
___

2. Since you can do all things through Christ who strengthens you, what are you not doing that you need to do? Why?
___
___
___

The Roots of Vision

3. Have you started a meaningful project or plan and it is still not done? Why?
   _____
   _____
   _____
   _____

4. Relative to moving forward in life, how does your vision become a reality?
   _____
   _____
   _____
   _____

5. What are you doing today that will cause God to say to you "Well done, you good and faithful servant?"
   _____
   _____
   _____
   _____

6. Have you shared you vision with anyone? Was it received with excitement or raised eyebrows? Why?
   _____
   _____
   _____
   _____

7. How would you know if someone is a good fit to work with you on your vision?
   _____
   _____
   _____
   _____

The Roots of Character

8. What would you do if you had unlimited financial resources?
_____
_____
_____
_____

9. How have you benefited from someone else's vision?
_____
_____
_____
_____

10. Why is a God given vision given to you not yours?
_____
_____
_____
_____

11. What inheritance are you leaving for your children's children?
_____
_____
_____
_____

12. Look back at you answer to question 8, was God's plan for your life considered in your response?
_____
_____
_____
_____

The Roots of Vision

MEMORY VERSES

Joel 2:28—I will pour out my Spirit on all people. Your sons and daughters will prophesy, your old men will dream dreams, your young men will see visions.

Habakkuk 2:2—Write down the revelation and make it plain on tablets so that a herald may run with it.

Psalms 62:11—One thing God has spoken, two things have I heard that you, O God, are strong.

The Roots of a Renewed Mind

The courting process of eagles has the appearance of a game. The female eagle flies around while the male eagle is in hot pursuit; at some point the female decides to raise the stakes in this *game*. She flies to the ground to retrieve a large stick and flies to ten thousand feet to drop it; this process repeats itself until she has a small stick and is flying around 500 feet in a tight figure eight. At some point, the male eagle has to realize that this is more than just a game, but is a test to see if he has a renewed mind. For at any point if the male eagle drops the stick, the *game* really was just a game and he lost. The female eagle will chase him away. If he changes from playing a game to treasuring her *stick*, then they would mate for life. See, the stick represents the unborn child or vision of the female and as long as his mind is keyed in to the subtle change that has occurred, a lifelong commitment is his earned reward.

1. What has to happen for you to change your mind? Why?
___
___
___
___

2. What is the dominant thought that runs through your mind? What are you saying to yourself?
___
___
___
___

The Roots of a Renewed Mind

3. Think of something that you continue to do even though you do not want to do it; now answer this, why do you keep doing it?
___
___
___
___

4. What do you think Satan wants from you the most? Does you current mindset cause you to unintentionally give in to the devil?
___
___
___
___

5. Think about something that you consider being *bad* that happened to you; what did you learn from it?
___
___
___
___

6. Would you have learned this life lesson outside of the happening?
___
___
___
___

7. Is it easier for you to learn the lesson after first failing?
___
___
___
___

8. When is the best time for you to grow?
_____
_____
_____

9. Does it matter why *it* happened? You get to define *it* for yourself.
_____
_____
_____

10. Do you know the power of forgiving? What happens to you if you do not forgive?
_____
_____
_____

11. Have you forgiven yourself?
_____
_____
_____

12. What is the difference between faith and fear? Why?
_____
_____
_____

The Roots of a Renewed Mind

MEMORY VERSES

2 Corinthians 5:17—Therefore, if anyone is in Christ, he is a new creation; the old has gone, the new has come!

2 Timothy 1:7—For God did not give us a spirit of fear, but of power, love and a sound mind.

Jeremiah 29:11—For I know the plans I have for you, declares the Lord, plans to prosper you and not harm you, and plans to give you hope and a future.

2 Corinthians 10:5—We demolish arguments and every pretension that sets itself up against the knowledge of God, and we take captive every thought to make it obedient to Christ.

The Roots of Giving

Priming the pump is an expression used to describe the process of using outside stimulus to provoke a desired response; economically, the government attempts to do this priming by cutting taxes for example. As it relates to giving, priming the pump is using your current resources to jump start the principle of reciprocity; as you give, it shall be given back to you.

1. Two things happen with a closed hand; first, you are not able to receive anything, what is the other? Who is hurt most by a closed hand?

   _____
   _____
   _____

2. What was Jesus after when he told the rich man to sell all his possessions? Why?

   _____
   _____
   _____

3. How do you present yourself to God?

   _____
   _____
   _____

The Roots of Giving

4. Have you ever given something and later regretted it? Why?
   _____
   _____
   _____
   _____

5. Should you give when you have more than enough or give out of your need? Why?
   _____
   _____
   _____
   _____

6. What does the giving of tithes and offerings say about your relationship with God?
   _____
   _____
   _____
   _____

7. What is the benefit of giving?
   _____
   _____
   _____
   _____

8. Are you ready to prosper? How do you know that you are ready?
   _____
   _____
   _____
   _____

The Roots of Character

9. Why would you have a feast or party?
_____
_____
_____

10. Is it easier to give your time or your money? Why?
_____
_____
_____

11. What is the greatest gift you have to give? Why?
_____
_____
_____

12. What does it mean to be a cheerful giver?
_____
_____
_____

MEMORY VERSES

Revelation 14:7—He said in a loud voice, "Fear God and give him the glory . . ."

2 Corinthians 9:7—Each man should give what he has decided in his heart to give, not reluctantly or under compulsion, for God loves a cheerful giver.

Acts 20:35—In everything I did, I showed you that by this kind of hard work we must help the weak, remembering the words the Lord Jesus himself said: "It is more blessed to give than to receive."

The Roots of Faith and Wisdom

One day while driving home, I drove over a half a brick that bounced off the pavement and hit my gas tank. I did not know that it put a whole in it, until the next morning as I was driving to work; another driver told me that my car was leaking gas as I sat on an incline. I drove back home called a friend of mine and then drove to the car dealership to get it repaired. It was only after being at the car dealership and the serviceman's refusal to drive the car did I realize the gravity of what I was doing. Driving a car with a whole in the gas tank is not wise and certainly was not a proper use of faith. Fortunately, my faith did allow for God to protect me in my ignorance.

1. Is your faith producing or productive?
_____
_____
_____
_____

2. What is it that you would like for God to do for you?
_____
_____
_____
_____

3. Are you quick to defend yourself if verbally attacked?
_____
_____
_____
_____

The Roots of Character

4. Could you stand in faith, even if you were standing alone?

5. How do you deliver bad news? Would the person say *thank you?*

6. Why do trials and troubles happen?

7. What limits have you placed on your faith? What would you not do?

8. Faith may bring you out of trouble, but what will keep you out? Why?

9. What do you use to fight the good fight of faith? Why?

The Roots of Faith and Wisdom

10. How do you get wisdom? What do you do with the wisdom that you have?
___
___
___
___

11. How does faith and wisdom work together for you? What happens if they do not work together?
___
___
___
___

12. What is the difference between faith and fantasy?
___
___
___
___

MEMORY VERSES

Proverbs 4:5—Get wisdom, get understanding; do not forget my words or swerve from them.

Proverbs 24:3-4—By wisdom a house is built, and through understanding it is established; through knowledge its rooms are filled with rare and beautiful treasures.

Proverbs 22:11—He who loves a pure heart and whose speech is gracious will have the king for his friend.

Hebrews 11:6—And without faith it is impossible to believe God, because anyone who comes to him must believe that he exists and that he rewards those who earnestly seek him.

Galatians 2:20—I have been crucified with Christ and I no longer live, but Christ lives in me. The life I live in the body, I live by faith in the Son of God, who loved me and gave himself for me.

James 2:26b—As the body without the spirit is dead, so faith without deeds is dead.

The Roots of Discipline

Adam and Elijah were asked revealing questions by God on the heels of their respective failures. After Adam ate of the tree, he tried to hide from God as he heard the Lord walking in the garden; God asked Adam, "Where are you?" After Elijah had called down fire from heaven and stopped rain to name a couple things, he ran to the mountain of God to escape Jezebel, who was determined to kill him. Once he was on the mountain, God asked him, "What are you doing here?" Both questions relate to a state of mind and are the result of a lack of discipline; Adam turned his back on God for woman and Elijah thought he was the only prophet left and had to save himself by running away. What an amazing set of events.

1. What are you doing here?

2. Where are you?

3. Have you given Satan power over you?

4. Why is it that not everyone can be on top?
_____
_____
_____

5. Do you know that your experiences were for your development and not a blueprint for the world?
_____
_____
_____

6. Are you waiting for God to part the waters?
_____
_____
_____

7. Are you your brother's keeper? Why or why not?
_____
_____
_____

8. What does it mean to be humble?
_____
_____
_____

9. How different are you when you are tired? Do you *love* the same when you are tired?
_____
_____
_____

The Roots of Discipline

10. After you have done all you can, what do you do next? Why?
___
___
___
___

11. How do you overcome your fear?
___
___
___
___

12. How long will you wait for something that you want? What do you want?
___
___
___
___

MEMORY VERSES

Hebrews 12:11—No discipline seems pleasant at the time, but painful. Later on, however, it produces a harvest of righteousness and peace for those who have been trained by it.

Revelation 3:19—Those whom I love I rebuke and discipline. So be earnest and repent.

Proverbs 13:18—He who ignores discipline comes to poverty and shame, but whoever heeds correction is honored.

The Roots of Impartation

Years ago, I received an impartation from the Lord through a vision. I was in church and saw myself down on my knees; in fact, I saw myself in the spot where I really was, but my view was from the other side of the sanctuary. I was standing in front of the pulpit near my pastor who was also looking at me as I was down on my knees. As I started to stand up, with my arms raised, a bright, white robe came down over me and I was clothed in righteousness. I still had and have a lot more to learn, but at least, I was on the right path and God said so to me and my pastor.

1. What was your personal encounter with God or an angel? What did you receive?

2. Can God get you without you experiencing him?

3. What is the benefit of having a mentor? Why?

The Roots of Impartation

4. Since faith comes by hearing, to what or whom are you listening?

5. Have you ever received a word of the Lord from someone? How did you know that it was God?

6. Would you take a test to see if you are insecure? What do you think the results would tell you?

7. What does it mean to be baptized with the Holy Spirit? Why is this necessary?

8. Do you know the voice of God? How?

The Roots of Character

9. Why is it important to not be in agreement in deception?

10. Do you realize that all things are possible if you believe? Why is this significant to your walk with God?

11. Through what ways have you received an impartation?

12. How does the rod of correction impart wisdom?

The Roots of Impartation

MEMORY VERSES

Acts 1:8—But you will receive power when the Holy Spirit come upon you; and you will be my witnesses in Jerusalem, and in all Judea and Samaria, and to the ends of the earth.

Acts 10:43—All the prophets testify about him that everyone who believes in him receives forgiveness of sins through his name.

Matthew 7:8—For everyone who asks receives; he who seeks finds; and to him who knocks, the door will opened.

The Roots of Leadership

A leadership exercise, studying a book, or even a letter of recommendation will not make you a leader; leadership is an interesting phenomenon in that you do not become a leader of men until you are followed; leadership, true leadership, is earned and pronounced by those who believe in you; the irony is the greater your leadership, the more you need to realized that it is not about you; more so, the attention or focus should not be on you, but rather on the one you serve.

1. Is a leader a person?

2. What is the difference between being an example and being a role model?

3. Who are you following? Why?

The Roots of Leadership

4. Who would win a battle between an army of sheep led by a lion and an army of lions led by a sheep? Why?
   _____
   _____
   _____
   _____

5. What does your answer to the previous question tell you about leadership?
   _____
   _____
   _____
   _____

6. Which of these is the greatest: an apostle, prophet, evangelist, pastor or teacher? Why?
   _____
   _____
   _____
   _____

7. Do you always follow the principles that you teach or have learned?
   _____
   _____
   _____
   _____

8. How do you respond when things do not go your way?
   _____
   _____
   _____
   _____

The Roots of Character

9. Are you a leader? How do you know?
_____
_____
_____

10. Why is it important to put your focus on God instead of man?
_____
_____
_____

11. Do you realize that your character speaks even before you open your mouth? Why is this so?
_____
_____
_____

12. Do you always tell the truth? What if the truth hurts?
_____
_____
_____

The Roots of Leadership

MEMORY VERSES

Joshua 1:8—Do not let this Book of the Law depart from your mouth; meditate on it day and night, so that you may be careful to do everything written in it. Then you will be prosperous and successful.

Romans 12:8—if it is encouraging, let him encourage; if it is contributing to the need of others, let him give generously; it is it leadership, let him govern diligently; if it is showing mercy, let him do it cheerfully.

John 10:3—The watchman opens the gate for him and the sheep listen to his voice. He calls his own sheep by name and leads them out.

The Roots of Development

1 Chronicles 4:9-10 "Jabez was more honorable than his brothers. His mother had named him Jabez, saying, 'I gave birth out of my pain.' Jabez cried out to the God of Israel, 'Oh that you would bless me and enlarge my territory! Let your hand be with me, keep me from harm so that I will be free from pain. And God granted his request.' The Prayer of Jabez is one of the most powerful prayers in the bible and clearly highlights the need to be fully developed. You have to be ready to have your tent enlarged.

1. What can you control? Why?

2. Not counting your children, who depends on you? Why?

3. Who do you depend on? Why?

The Roots of Development

4. Would it be best to be in a relationship where both parties depend on each other? Why?
___
___
___
___

5. What types of people are drawn to you? Why?
___
___
___
___

6. Have you or do you imitate others? Why?
___
___
___
___

7. How often do you seek personal growth? Are you satisfied with this amount of time? Why or why not?
___
___
___
___

8. Are you the same person you were five or ten years ago? How?
___
___
___
___

9. Have you ever hindered someone's development? How?
___
___
___
___

The Roots of Character

10. What should you do when you are wrongly accused? Why?
_____
_____
_____

11. What should you do to control your anxiety for something that you really want?
_____
_____
_____

12. Do you understand why prayer is necessary? What is the purpose of prayer?
_____
_____
_____

MEMORY VERSES

Revelation 2:10—Do not be afraid of what you are about to suffer, I tell you, the devil will put some of you in prison to test you, and you will suffer persecution for ten days.

Isaiah 60:22—The least of you will become a thousand, the smallest a mighty nation. I am the Lord; in its time I will do this swiftly.

Philippians 4:6—Do not be anxious about anything, but in everything, by prayer and petition, with thanksgiving, present your requests to God.

Remembering Your Roots

2 Chronicles 7:14-15 reads, "If my people, who are called by my name will humble themselves and pray and seek my face and turn from their wicked ways, then will I hear from heaven and will forgive their sin and will heal their land. Now my eyes will be open and my ears attentive to the prayers offered in this place." You are the *land* and a recipient of that promise; all you have to do it meet the condition.

1. Why does God accept you just as you are?
   _____
   _____
   _____
   _____

2. Can you remember a hurtful or painful situation without reliving it?
   _____
   _____
   _____
   _____

3. When does the memory of the above situation come to your mind? Why do you think this is?
   _____
   _____
   _____
   _____

The Roots of Character

4. Do you accept that the Lord will give you rest? Why?
   _____
   _____
   _____
   _____

5. Do you realize that you have a choice about everything? Why?
   _____
   _____
   _____
   _____

6. How do you take ownership of your pain?
   _____
   _____
   _____
   _____

7. What does it mean to you to be bought by the blood of Jesus?
   _____
   _____
   _____
   _____

8. What did Christ do for you? What are you doing for him?
   _____
   _____
   _____
   _____

9. What does it mean for God to say that you are his?
   _____
   _____
   _____
   _____

Remembering Your Roots

10. Can you relate to God as your Father? Why?
_____
_____
_____
_____

11. Why is it important to remember the events of the last supper?
_____
_____
_____
_____

12. Surely God has and is blessing you, do you thank him for the things he has already done?
_____
_____
_____
_____

MEMORY VERSES

Luke 23:34—Father, forgive them, for they do not know what they are doing.

John 19: 30—When he had received the drink, Jesus said, "It is finished." With that, he bowed his head and gave up his spirit.

Romans 8:38-39—For I am convinced that neither death nor life, neither angels nor demons, neither the present nor the future, nor any powers, neither height nor depth, nor anything else in all creation, will be able to separate us from the love of God that is in Christ Jesus our Lord.

1 John 4:4—You, dear children, are from God and have overcome them, because the one who is in you is greater than the one who is in the world.

The Beginning

Jeremiah 1:5a reads, "Before I formed you in the womb, I knew you, before you were born I set you apart." Your beginning did not start when you were born; this scripture says that we were in heaven with God; it says that God knows us better than we know ourselves; it says that God has a plan for sending us to earth; we just have to do our part in submitting to him, reading His word and developing in Christ. We were born with a purpose, now we just need to begin to carry it out.

1. Do you need to be reminded of things that are your responsibility? Why?

2. Are you willing to be embarrassed for Christ?

3. Did you know that doing what is right now can override the mistakes of your past?

4. Are you in the right position for growth? How do you know?
   _____
   _____
   _____
   _____

5. What happens to you when you call upon God?
   _____
   _____
   _____
   _____

6. How do you make your new growth last?
   _____
   _____
   _____
   _____

7. Why was the earth formless and void after God created it?
   _____
   _____
   _____
   _____

8. Do you know that God promised to do a new thing in you? What does that cause you to think about?
   _____
   _____
   _____
   _____

9. What does it mean to you that Jesus is the same yesterday, today and forevermore?
   _____
   _____
   _____
   _____

The Beginning

10. Have you ever done everything that you were supposed to do and still not succeed? What did you do next?
   _____
   _____
   _____
   _____

11. If you have two things before you and do not know which will work, what should you do? Why?
   _____
   _____
   _____
   _____

12. When someone does something that is a surprise, do you assess their character before drawing conclusions?
   _____
   _____
   _____
   _____

MEMORY VERSES

Ephesians 5:8—For once you were darkness, but now you are the light in the Lord. Live as children of light.

Philippians 4:13—I can do everything through him who gives me strength.

Romans 1:16a—I am not ashamed of the gospel, because it is the power of God for the salvation to everyone who believes

Real Life Scenarios

The following are real life scenarios for you to ponder or better yet, to begin to put your newly formed or developing character to the test. Take you time and as always, be truthful in your responses.

1. The Vice President of Operations at your place of employment asks you to do something that you know is beyond your skill level. Do you admit that you do not know how to do it?

   _____
   _____
   _____
   _____

2. Someone has done a really mean and malicious thing to you and it caused you great discomfort and pain. You have knowledge that this person is about to get hurt by unknowingly using faulty equipment. You have knowledge of this *mild* danger. Do you warn the person?

   _____
   _____
   _____
   _____

3. Your electric company bills you ten dollars but your average bill normally is one hundred dollars. You have

Real Life Scenarios

not changed your service nor adjusted your usage. Do you notify the company of the possible error?

4. To avoid paying a hefty fine or to escape great personal or family embarrassment or to avoid having your privileges taken away a person of authority asks for *favor* in lieu of this punishment. Would you do this favor?

5. Your boss asks you do something that is extremely and personally important. Time passes and you have not done it; upon being asked about it, do you tell your boss that you have not done it?

6. You are on an international trip carrying expensive equipment once you get to customs there is a two thousand dollar fee to enter the country with the equipment. Subsequently, you learn that you could give the customs agent one hundred dollars and he would let you through. Would you give the agent the hundred dollars?

7. A procedural error was made in a complex assignment; you have completed this work and it would be heavily involved, time consuming and costly to correct the error? Would you fix the error?

8. It is 3:00 a.m. You are on your way home and are extremely tired after a long, stressful day. As you are nearing home, you get caught at a red light that is really, really long. There are no other cars around and the road is clear. Do you carefully drive through the red light?

9. A friend offers you the use their employee discount to get a reduced price on clothing. You are not an employee. Do you use the employee discount?

10. You have been looking for a job, but have been turned down based on being over qualified. You found another opportunity and desperately need a job. Would you understate your qualifications to get this job?

Real Life Scenarios

11. You are returning an item to the store that was purchased on sale; the clerk is not paying attention and refunds you the full price of the item. Do you bring it to the clerk's attention?

___

12. You have direct knowledge of a coworker's mistake. This employee has a reputation of making a lot of mistakes and had just made a major blunder the week before. This current mistake is just as serious. Do you tell your supervisor about the error?

___

The Roots of Character

As stated or alluded to, this is not the end but rather the beginning and I hope that every day you make the right choice. I now leave you with these final thoughts, and yes, I begin with trees.

Even when a tree appears to be fully grown, mature and producing there is simultaneous growth in its roots. As it branches out, its roots continue to grow; as it produces fruit, season after season, its roots continue to grow. The last chapter of the main text is entitled *The Beginning;* this is because everyday there is a new opportunity to build, hopefully a resolve to be a better person and to succeed in God. Everyday you begin again; be mindful that you are not starting over, but rather you are getting a fresh new perspective and energy in which to tackle the day. See, God's mercy is renewed everyday for God knows that you may not always get it right, but his desire is that you never give up and that you should always continue to pursue the righteousness of God. God loves you and love covers a multitude of sin; God heals you for the pains of life are byproducts of living; God saves because there are some things that you can not do for yourself. My hope is that this book will become a platform for your development; that you will refer to it over and over again as you develop; again, the key thing to remember is that as you continue to grow, your roots will continue to grow.

Real Life Scenarios

I leave you with this prayer . . .

Father in the name of the Lord Jesus Christ I pray that your servant, the reader, will embrace the love of God and gravitate toward a daily walk in the character of Christ. Lord Jesus I pray for your friend, the reader, that the hope of Christ and peace of God shall be the prevailing spirit that lives in them. I pray that your disciple, the reader, will become a permanent student of righteousness and fulfill their purpose in God. May the Lord Jesus Christ bless you richly in your desire to develop into a great man or woman of God. I bless your walk with the Lord to be covered by peace of God. Finally, may the grace of the Lord Jesus Christ, and the love of God, and the fellowship of the Holy Spirit be with you all your days; in Jesus' name. Amen.

Recommended reading:

The Logic of Faith:
A Journey of Understanding
by Antonio L. McDaniel

Behold, I give you faith! Now, you have the ability to move and live and breathe in confidence; that everything you touch will work; all that you think about will become a positive influence and change lives; you will even become wealthy in the process. Clearly, it would be absolutely wonderful for God to make that pronouncement to you and it becomes so. Fortunately, and to what may be the ultimate paradox, this kind of mature faith will only come by trials, perseverance, and yes, an experiential journey that is a natural occurrence of life. Faith increases as it is used and grows exponentially when it is tested. The true depth of these *tests of faith* does not come because you decide to seek or pursue God more; these tests come because *faith* is alive and demands to be fed, even challenged. Admittedly, faith does appear to be somewhat illogical, but most goals or feats of greatness are often questioned or met with resistance; in the end, when the goal has been met, the feat obtained and the journey completed, it is only then, in clear hindsight that you realize that this was a test of your faith; subsequently, as you reflect on your travels, you think about all the things that you would have changed or done differently, only to later realize that if things were different you may not be who you are or fulfill your purpose in God. The Logic of Faith is a reasonable step along your current path; through personal experiences, some good, some not so good, I share my trials of faith,

Dedication

so you can be enlightened and encouraged as you continue on your journey of understanding. Once you embrace and unite with your faith, the world will truly become your oyster and it will not matter where you are or what you are facing.